First World War
and Army of Occupation
War Diary
France, Belgium and Germany

58 DIVISION
Headquarters, Branches and Services
Commander Royal Artillery
21 January 1917 - 5 December 1918

WO95/2992/4

The Naval & Military Press Ltd
www.nmarchive.com
Published in association with The National Archives

Published by

The Naval & Military Press Ltd

Unit 10 Ridgewood Industrial Park,

Uckfield, East Sussex,

TN22 5QE England

Tel: +44 (0) 1825 749494

www.naval-military-press.com

www.nmarchive.com

This diary has been reprinted in facsimile from the original. Any imperfections are inevitably reproduced and the quality may fall short of modern type and cartographic standards.

© Crown Copyright
Images reproduced by permission of The National Archives, London, England, 2015.

Contents

Document type	Place/Title	Date From	Date To
Heading	WO95/2992/4		
Heading	58 Division Troops C.R.A 1917 Jan-1918 Dec		
Heading	58 Division C.R.A 1917 Jan-1918 Dec		
War Diary	Heytesbury	21/01/1917	21/01/1917
War Diary	Southampton	21/01/1917	21/01/1917
War Diary	Havre	22/01/1917	22/01/1917
War Diary	Beauvoir Wavans	24/01/1917	24/01/1917
War Diary	Rucheux	05/02/1917	05/02/1917
War Diary	Henu	26/02/1917	01/03/1917
War Diary	Bavincourt	28/03/1917	28/03/1917
War Diary	La Cauchie	13/04/1917	13/04/1917
War Diary	Gomiecourt	22/04/1917	22/04/1917
Heading	War Diary Of 58th H.Q. R.A From 3/5/17 To 29/5/17		
War Diary		03/05/1917	29/05/1917
Heading	War Diary Of C.R.A 58 Division From 1/6/17 To 30/6/17 Vol 6		
War Diary		08/06/1917	31/07/1917
War Diary	Hauteville	01/08/1917	26/08/1917
War Diary	Reninghelst	26/08/1917	03/09/1917
War Diary	Ypres	05/09/1917	31/10/1917
Operation(al) Order(s)	58th Divisional Artillery Group Order No. 49	28/10/1917	28/10/1917
Operation(al) Order(s)	58th Divisional Artillery Order No. 45	24/10/1917	24/10/1917
Miscellaneous	58th Divisional Artillery Group	27/10/1917	27/10/1917
Operation(al) Order(s)	58th Divisional Artillery Group Order No. 51	28/10/1917	28/10/1917
Operation(al) Order(s)	58th Divisional Artillery Group Order No. 55	03/11/1917	03/11/1917
Miscellaneous	Barrage Table		
War Diary	Ypres	31/10/1917	18/11/1917
Operation(al) Order(s)	58th Divisional Artillery Group Order No. 56	04/11/1917	04/11/1917
Miscellaneous	Barrage Table "A"		
Miscellaneous	Table "B"		
Operation(al) Order(s)	58th Divisional Artillery Order No. 57	05/11/1917	05/11/1917
Miscellaneous	Barrage Table 'A'		
Operation(al) Order(s)	58th Divisional Artillery Group Order No. 58	05/11/1917	05/11/1917
Operation(al) Order(s)	58th Divisional Artillery Group Order No. 59	06/11/1917	06/11/1917
Miscellaneous	Amendment To 58th D.A Group Order No. 59	06/11/1917	06/11/1917
Operation(al) Order(s)	58th Divisional Artillery Group Order No. 60	06/11/1917	06/11/1917
Miscellaneous	Barrage Table A 1		
Miscellaneous	Barrage Table A 2		
Miscellaneous	Table "B" Issued With 58th D.A. Group Order No. 60	30/10/1917	30/10/1917
Operation(al) Order(s)	58th Divisional Artillery Group Order No. 61	06/11/1917	06/11/1917
Operation(al) Order(s)	58th Divisional Artillery Group Order No. 62	07/11/1917	07/11/1917
Operation(al) Order(s)	58th Divisional Artillery Group Order No. 63	08/11/1917	08/11/1917
Miscellaneous	Barrage Table "A"		
Operation(al) Order(s)	58th Divisional Artillery Group Order No. 65	09/11/1917	09/11/1917
Miscellaneous	Barrage Table "A"	09/11/1917	09/11/1917
Miscellaneous	Addendum No.1 To 58th D.A. Group Order No. 65	09/11/1917	09/11/1917
Operation(al) Order(s)	58th Divisional Artillery Group Order No. 66	09/11/1917	09/11/1917
Operation(al) Order(s)	58th Divisional Artillery Group Order No. 68	12/11/1917	12/11/1917
Miscellaneous	Barrage Table		

Type	Description	Start	End
Miscellaneous	Amendment To 58th Divisional Arty. Group Order No. 67, Appendix I And 58th D.A Group Order No. 68	12/11/1917	12/11/1917
Operation(al) Order(s)	58th Divisional Artillery Group Order No. 69	14/11/1917	14/11/1917
Operation(al) Order(s)	58th Divisional Artillery Group Order No. 72	16/11/1917	16/11/1917
Operation(al) Order(s)	58th Divisional Artillery Group Order No. 73	16/11/1917	16/11/1917
Operation(al) Order(s)	58th Divisional Artillery Group Order No. 74	17/11/1917	17/11/1917
Miscellaneous	Location Statement Of No.2 Group 1st (imperial) D.A Group		
War Diary	Etaples Area	04/12/1917	15/12/1917
War Diary	Canal Bank South Of Boesinghe	01/01/1918	31/01/1918
War Diary	HQ Rouez Front Vendeuil La. Fere Barisis	01/02/1918	28/02/1918
War Diary		03/02/1918	15/02/1918
War Diary	Quierzy	01/03/1918	24/03/1918
War Diary	Camelin	24/03/1918	26/03/1918
War Diary	Blerancourt	27/03/1918	31/03/1918
Heading	War Diary Headquarters 58th Divisional Artillery April 1918		
War Diary	Blerancourt	01/04/1918	04/04/1918
War Diary	Cagny	04/04/1918	07/04/1918
War Diary	Boves	08/04/1918	13/04/1918
War Diary	Fort Manior Farm	14/04/1918	30/04/1918
War Diary	Francieres	01/05/1918	16/05/1918
War Diary	Contay	17/05/1918	02/06/1918
War Diary	Bavelincourt	07/06/1918	08/06/1918
War Diary	Argoeuves	10/06/1918	20/06/1918
War Diary	Beaucourt	21/06/1918	31/07/1918
Heading	58th Divl. Artillery C.R.A 58th Division August 1918		
War Diary	Beau Court	01/08/1918	04/08/1918
War Diary	Querrieu	06/08/1918	07/08/1918
War Diary	J.9.c.9.3.	08/08/1918	08/08/1918
War Diary	J.26.	12/08/1918	30/08/1918
Miscellaneous	Precis Of Operations From 8th To 12th August 1918		
Miscellaneous	58th Division	15/08/1918	15/08/1918
Miscellaneous	Precis Of Operations From 8th To 12th August 1918		
Miscellaneous	Narrative Of Events From 25th August To 1st September 1918		
Operation(al) Order(s)	58th Divisional Artillery Order No. 150	05/08/1918	05/08/1918
Miscellaneous	Table "A" (58th D.A Order No. 150)		
Miscellaneous	Amendment No.1 To 58th D.A. Order No. 150	06/08/1918	06/08/1918
Miscellaneous	Amendment No.3 To 58th D.A. Order No. 150	07/08/1918	07/08/1918
Diagram etc	Diagram		
Operation(al) Order(s)	58th Divisional Artillery Order No. 151	06/08/1918	06/08/1918
Map	Map		
Operation(al) Order(s)	58th Divisional Artillery Order No. 153	09/08/1918	09/08/1918
Map	Map		
Diagram etc	Diagram		
Operation(al) Order(s)	58th Divisional Artillery Order No. 154	09/08/1918	09/08/1918
Operation(al) Order(s)	58th Divisional Artillery Order No. 155	25/08/1918	25/08/1918
Operation(al) Order(s)	58th Divisional Artillery Order No. 156	26/08/1918	26/08/1918
Operation(al) Order(s)	58th Divisional Artillery Group Order No. 157	26/08/1918	26/08/1918
Miscellaneous	Bde. R.F.A.	27/08/1918	27/08/1918
Operation(al) Order(s)	58th Divisional Artillery Order No. 158	27/08/1918	27/08/1918
Diagram etc	Diagram		
Operation(al) Order(s)	58th Divisional Artillery Order No. 159	27/08/1918	27/08/1918
Operation(al) Order(s)	58th Divisional Artillery Order No. 160	28/08/1918	28/08/1918
Operation(al) Order(s)	58th Divisional Artillery Order No. 161	26/08/1918	26/08/1918

Type	Description	Date From	Date To
Diagram etc	Diagram		
Miscellaneous	Amendment No.1 To 58th D.A Order No. 161	28/08/1918	28/08/1918
Operation(al) Order(s)	58th Divisional Artillery Order No. 162	29/08/1918	29/08/1918
Miscellaneous	Messages And Signals		
Operation(al) Order(s)	58th Divisional Artillery Order No. 163	30/08/1918	30/08/1918
Operation(al) Order(s)	58th Divisional Artillery Order No. 164	31/08/1918	31/08/1918
Miscellaneous	86th Army Bde. R.F.A.	28/08/1918	28/08/1918
Miscellaneous	86th Army Bde R.F.A.	29/08/1918	29/08/1918
Miscellaneous	Sandford's Group	30/08/1918	30/08/1918
Miscellaneous	58th Divisional Artillery Group Location Statement	26/08/1918	26/08/1918
Miscellaneous	58th Divisional Artillery Location Statement	28/08/1918	28/08/1918
Miscellaneous	58th Divisional Artillery Location Statement	01/09/1918	01/09/1918
Heading	War Diary 58th D.A Sept 1918 Vol 21		
War Diary	A.19.b.8.0 Carnoy	01/09/1918	01/09/1918
War Diary	Railhead	01/09/1918	02/09/1918
War Diary	A.19.b.8.0 Carnoy	03/09/1918	07/09/1918
War Diary	D.22.a.4.1	08/09/1918	30/09/1918
Miscellaneous	Brigade Major, III Corps H.A	07/09/1918	07/09/1918
Operation(al) Order(s)	58th Divisional Artillery Order No. 165	01/09/1918	01/09/1918
Miscellaneous	Appendix "A" Heavy Artillery.		
Miscellaneous	Amendments No.1 To 58th D.A Order No. 165	01/09/1918	01/09/1918
Operation(al) Order(s)	58th Divisional Artillery Order No. 166	06/09/1918	06/09/1918
Operation(al) Order(s)	58th Divisional Artillery Order No. 167	08/09/1918	08/09/1918
Operation(al) Order(s)	58th Divisional Artillery Order No. 168	09/09/1918	09/09/1918
Miscellaneous	Appendix "A"		
Diagram etc	Diagram		
Miscellaneous	290th Brigade R.F.A.	10/09/1918	10/09/1918
Miscellaneous	290th Brigade R.F.A.	11/09/1918	11/09/1918
Operation(al) Order(s)	58th Divisional Artillery Order No. 169	11/09/1918	11/09/1918
Miscellaneous	A Form Messages And Signals		
Miscellaneous	290th Brigade R.F.A.	16/09/1918	16/09/1918
Miscellaneous	Addendum No.1 To 58th D.A Order No. 170	16/09/1918	16/09/1918
Operation(al) Order(s)	58th Divisional Artillery Order No. 170	16/09/1918	16/09/1918
Miscellaneous	Appendix "A"		
Diagram etc	Tracing 'A'		
Diagram etc	Tracing B		
Diagram etc	Tracing C		
Diagram etc	Tracing G		
Miscellaneous	G.S.O.2		
Miscellaneous	To All Recipients Of 58th D.A Order No. 170	17/09/1918	17/09/1918
Miscellaneous	Amendment No.1 To 58th D.A Order No. 170	17/09/1918	17/09/1918
Miscellaneous	290th Brigade R.F.A.	17/09/1918	17/09/1918
Operation(al) Order(s)	58th Divisional Artillery Order No. 171	22/09/1918	22/09/1918
Operation(al) Order(s)	58th Divisional Artillery Order No. 172	23/09/1918	23/09/1918
Miscellaneous	A Form Messages And Signals		
Operation(al) Order(s)	58th Divisional Artillery Order No. 173	23/09/1918	23/09/1918
War Diary	H.Q.R.A.	01/10/1918	01/10/1918
War Diary	D.22.a.2.4	01/10/1918	10/10/1918
War Diary	Hersin Coupigny Chateau	11/10/1918	12/10/1918
War Diary	Maroc	13/10/1918	13/10/1918
War Diary	O.23.b.5.6.	14/10/1918	18/10/1918
War Diary	Bersee	19/10/1918	20/10/1918
War Diary	Lannay	21/10/1918	01/11/1918
War Diary	H.3.b.80.20	01/11/1918	02/11/1918
War Diary	Lannay	03/11/1918	08/11/1918
War Diary	Bleharies	09/11/1918	09/11/1918

War Diary	Wiers	10/11/1918	10/11/1918
War Diary	Beloeil	11/11/1918	17/11/1918
War Diary	Peruwelz	21/11/1918	30/11/1918
Operation(al) Order(s)	58th Divisional Artillery Operation Order No. 186	01/11/1918	01/11/1918
Miscellaneous	Appendices		
Miscellaneous	Appendix "B" Smoke Screen and other Tasks for 4.5" Howitzers.		
Miscellaneous	Appendix "C"		
Miscellaneous	Heavy Artillery Support required by 58th Division for proposed operation. Appendix D		
Miscellaneous	Ammunition to be dumped at positions. Appendix "E"		
War Diary	Peruwelz Belgium	02/12/1918	05/12/1918

WO 95/2992/4

58 DIVISION. TROOPS

C.R.A

1917 JAN — 1918 DEC

Box 2860

58 DIVISION

CRA

1917 JAN — 1918 DEC

H.Q.R.A 58th Div

WAR DIARY
or
INTELLIGENCE SUMMARY.

Army Form C.2118
WR R a 5 8 7 D
Vol 1

Place	Date	Hour	Summary of Events and Information	Remarks and references to Appendices
Abergavenny	21/1/17	12:30p	Headquarters left for Southampton	
Southampton	21/1/17	5.0pm	Embarked for France	
Havre	22/1/17	9.30am	Entered Rest Camp at Havre. Left Havre 23/1/17	
Beauval Hauts	24/1/17	4pm	Occupied billets at Beauval Hauts	

C. M. Khan, Lieut.
for Reconnaissance Officer
58th Divisional Artillery

HQ RA 5th Div.

HQ RA 5th Div Army Form C. 2118.
Vol 2

WAR DIARY
or
INTELLIGENCE SUMMARY.
(Erase heading not required.)

Instructions regarding War Diaries and Intelligence Summaries are contained in F. S. Regs., Part II. and the Staff Manual respectively. Title pages will be prepared in manuscript.

Place	Date	Hour	Summary of Events and Information	Remarks and references to Appendices
Rucheux	5/2/19	3pm	Left Beaurainville 9.30am arrived & occupied billets at Rucheux	
Hem	26/2/19	1.30p	Left Rucheux 10.30am. Occupied billets at Hem	

C.M.Kilroy Lieut
for Reconnaissance Officer
5th Divisional Artillery

WAR DIARY WO RA 58 D Vol 3
or
INTELLIGENCE SUMMARY.

Army Form C. 2118.

(Erase heading not required.)

Place	Date	Hour	Summary of Events and Information	Remarks and references to Appendices
	1917			
HENU	13/16	10.30am	Moved to BAVINCOURT and occupied Billets	

HQRA
28.3.14

J.G. Ash.
Lieut. Recon. Officer
53rd Divisional Artillery

WAR DIARY
or
INTELLIGENCE SUMMARY.
(Erase heading not required.)

Army Form C. 2118.

HQ R.A. 58D Vol 4

Place	Date	Hour	Summary of Events and Information	Remarks and references to Appendices
BAVINCOURT	March 28th	1917	Headquarters moved to LA CAUCHIE	
	March 29th		The Divisional Artillery were attached to 21st Division with the 291st Bde. on the right H.Q's MOYENVILLE 290th Bde. on left, H.Q's at BOIRY forming parts of two groups.	
	April 2nd		The 21st Division attacked at 5.15 a.m. which was successful.	
	" 3rd		Batteries of each Brigade moved to forward positions to cover subsequent attack on afternoon and east staff of 9th of April of Hindenburg Line. Employed cutting wire.	
	April 9th		This attack was only partly successful.	
	April 15th		Headquarters moved from LA CAUCHIE to GOMIECOURT and the Brigades went into action near ECOUST to support the 62nd Division under C.R.A. 62nd Division.	
	April 22nd		Headquarters moved to join Divisional Headquarters at BIHUCOURT. During this period, our Batteries in the valley behind ECOUST were frequently heavily shelled. The defences of BULLECOURT were regularly bombarded.	
	April 27th		Major H.N.H.Williamson joined for duty as Brigade Major vice Major D.C.Wilson, R.A. *During this period the Brigades formed one Group under Lt. Col. H.N. Clark, only 290th Bde. R.F.A.*	

H.Q.R.A.
28.4.1917.

S M Reel
Brigadier General, R.A.
Commanding, 58th Divisional Artillery.

Army Form C. 2118.

WAR DIARY
or
INTELLIGENCE SUMMARY

H.Q. 58th Divisional Artillery.

(Erase heading not required.)

APRIL, 1917.

Vol 4

Instructions regarding War Diaries and Intelligence Summaries are contained in F. S. Regs., Part II. and the Staff Manual respectively. Title pages will be prepared in manuscript.

Place	Date	Hour	Summary of Events and Information	Remarks and references to Appendices
BAVINCOURT	23.3.17		58th Divisional Artillery attached to 21st Division for tactical purposes. Headquarters moved to LA CAUCHIE.	
LA CAUCHIE	3.4.17		58th Divisional Artillery ceased to be attached to 21st Division and attached to 62nd Division. Headquarters moved to GOMIECOURT.	
GOMIECOURT	22.4.17		Headquarters moved to BIHUCOURT.	

Lieut.
A.D.C., 58th Divisional Artillery.

Vol 5

CONFIDENTIAL
****

WAR DIARY

OF

58th Bde R.A.

From 3/5/17
To 29/5/17

Army Form C. 2118.

WAR DIARY
or
INTELLIGENCE SUMMARY. H.Q.R.A. 58th Division.

(Erase heading not required.)

Instructions regarding War Diaries and Intelligence Summaries are contained in F. S. Regs., Part II. and the Staff Manual respectively. Title pages will be prepared in manuscript.

Place	Date	Hour	Summary of Events and Information	Remarks and references to Appendices
	3- 5- 17.	3-30	Our batteries supported the attack by the 185th Brigade - 62nd Division - on BULLECOURT. The operation was a failure, although the N. objective was taken at first, but only to be lost again within two hours. The attack was continued on the day following, but also without success.	
	5- 5- 17.		Batteries of this Divisional Artillery came under the orders of B.G.R.A. 7th Division.	
	7- 5- 17.	3-45	The attack on BULLECOURT was renewed by the 20th Brigade (7th Division), and our batteries barraged in support. Slight progress was made as also on the following day. A third attack was made on 9-5-17, but was unsuccessful and by the evening the Brigade were back on their original line of the 7th.	
	14- 5- 17.		Between the 10th and 14th several other attempts to advance were made, but no appreciable progress resulted.	
	15- 5- 17.		174th Infantry Brigade (58th Division) came into the line.	
	16- 5- 17.		G.O.C. 58th Division assumed command, and 290, 291, 310 and 312th Brigades came under the command of the B.G. R.A. 58th Division, with Headquarters at MORY.	
	17- 5- 17.	2-a.m.	2/5th Battalion, 174th Infantry Brigade attacked and captured the whole of the village of BULLECOURT. The enemy remained in possession of the support line to the North of the village.	

T.J.34. Wt. W708-776. 500000. 4/15. Sir J. C. & S.

Army Form C. 2118.

WAR DIARY
or
INTELLIGENCE SUMMARY.
(Erase heading not required.)

Instructions regarding War Diaries and Intelligence Summaries are contained in F. S. Regs., Part II. and the Staff Manual respectively. Title pages will be prepared in manuscript.

Place	Date	Hour	Summary of Events and Information	Remarks and references to Appendices
	21-5-17.	3-45	An attack was made on BOVIS trench, the trench North of village. Our troops took the objective, but overstepping it, were driven back by enemy who were strongly holding a line of shell holes behind. Throughout the period our Artillery has kept the enemy's communication and centres of activity under fire.	
	29.5.17.	9 a.m.	The two Brigades of the 7th Divisional Artillery, i.e. 22nd and 35th F.A. Bdes., came under the command of the B.G.R.A., 58th Division.	

H.Q.R.A.
29/5/1917.

Brigadier General, R.A.
Commanding, 58th Divisional Artillery.

Vol 56 ✱

Confidential

War Diary
of
CRA 58 Division
from 1/4/17 to 30/6/17

Army Form C. 2118.

WAR DIARY
or
INTELLIGENCE SUMMARY.
(Erase heading not required.)

Headquarters, 58th Divisional Artl.

Instructions regarding War Diaries and Intelligence Summaries are contained in F.S. Regs., Part II. and the Staff Manual respectively. Title pages will be prepared in manuscript.

Place	Date	Hour	Summary of Events and Information	Remarks and references to Appendices
	8/6/17.	11.30p.m.	Our batteries supported the 173rd Infantry Brigade in a successful raid made on enemy's trenches in MU.14.c. securing one prisoner and inflicting several casualties. The hostile barrage came down at 11.38 but was only of slight intensity.	
	14/6/17.	2.0. a.m.	The 175th Infantry Brigade successfully raided the BOVIS trench between U22d50.40. and U.22.6.20.50 and our batteries barraged in support. Two prisoners and one machine gun were captured, and several casualties inflicted.	
	15/6/17.	2.50. a.m.	An attack was made on the HINDENBURG front line between U.20.b.40.20. and U.14.c.30.90.' and a strong point at cross roads U.14.c.36,95. by the 173rd Infantry Brigade and was supported by a barrage from our batteries. Our troops gained their objectives everywhere excepting a Mebu, and captured 41 prisoners. the enemy made numerous counter attacks and recaptured a small portion on the Hindenburg front line the following evening.	
	16/6/17.	3.10.a.m.	The 173rd Infantry Brigade Attacked the Hindenburg support line, after first retaking portion of front line, between U. 20.b.50.70. and U.14.a.40.50. and were supported by our batteries. The objective was gained, but our troops were eventually forced to retire to the Hindenburg front line owing to the enemy's superior numbers.	
	24/6/17.	10.0.a.m.	The B.G.RA. 7th Division took over command of 290th and 291st Brigades, while in the line from B.G.R.A. 58th Division. R.A.H.Q. moved to COURCELLES.	
28/29/6/17.			Batteries relieved by 7th Division, moved to wagon lines.	
			During this month the batteries have been under constant heavy shell fire in the ECOUST VALLEY.	

H.Williams Bgt m. R.A.
Brigadier General, R.A.
Commanding, 58th Divisional Artillery.

Army Form C. 2118.

WAR DIARY
or
INTELLIGENCE SUMMARY.
(Erase heading not required.)

Headquarters, 58th Divisional Artillery.

Instructions regarding War Diaries and Intelligence Summaries are contained in F.S. Regs., Part II. and the Staff Manual respectively. Title pages will be prepared in manuscript.

Vol 7

Place	Date	Hour	Summary of Events and Information	Remarks and references to Appendices
	4/7/17.		R.A.H.Q. moved from COURCELLES - LE - COMTE to MEAULTE.	
	5/7/17. to 6/7/17.		290th Brigade R.F.A. of 58th Divisional Artillery relieved 157th Brigade R.F.A. in the line passing under the command of the B.G.R.A. 59th Division.	
	10/7/17.	10 a.m.	Command of 42nd Divisional Artillery and of 290th Brigade R.F.A. in the line passed to B.G.R.A. 58th Division, at YTRES.	
	7/7/17. to 27/7/17.		Our Batteries conducted a systematic bombardment of the enemy's advanced work on PLUSH TRENCH and forward areas generally, and supported the 173rd, 174th and 175th Infantry Brigades in a number of minor operations against the enemy's outposts, on the HAVRINCOURT front.	
	26/7/17.		Command of 210th Brigade R.F.A. of 42nd Division (less one Battery) reinforced by one section of the 211th Brigade R.F.A. of that Division, passed to B.G.R.A., 3rd Division.	
	28/29/7/17.		Our Batteries supported the 173rd Infantry Brigade in a raid on PLUSH TRENCH, which was found to be unoccupied.	
	31/7/17.		The command of the Divisional Artillery in the line passed to B.G.R.A., 9th Division. R.A.H.Q. moved from YTRES to HAUTEVILLE.	

SPReed
Brigadier General, R.A.
Commanding 58th Divisional Artillery.

WAR DIARY
or
INTELLIGENCE SUMMARY.

(Erase heading not required.)

Army Form C. 2118.

HQ RA 5-8 Vol 8

Place	Date	Hour	Summary of Events and Information	Remarks and references to Appendices
HAZEBROUCK	1-5-17		Divisional Artillery Headquarters handed over to 90 D.A. and moved to HAUTEVILLE 90 C Brigade went into action at MENNEL under orders of CRA 60 Division. 55 Brigade went into action in the vicinity of ST LEGER under orders of CRA, 21st Division.	
	20/5		Lt Col Baker was on leave from a/a to 27/5/17. In his august Mr Mohan was in Command.	
	26-5-17		Entrainment at ARMS of Divisional Artillery on route from Third to Fifth Army began. Units detrained at HOPOUTRE and GODEWAERSVELDE and went into staging area at RENINGHELST.	
RENINGHELST				Signed [signature] By Col RS CRA 50 Div

WAR DIARY or INTELLIGENCE SUMMARY

AO RA 58 Army Form C.2118

Place	Date	Hour	Summary of Events and Information	Remarks and references to Appendices
RENINGHELST	3-9-17		The batteries of this Divisional Artillery began to relieve batteries of 2nd Aust. D.A. in action by Zouave Wood under orders of C.R.A. 4th Division. This order was cancelled and batteries ordered to return to XVIII Corps.	
YPRES	5-9-17		Divisional Artillery joined Division in XVIII Corps area. HQ was established at BRAKE CAMP near VLAMERTINGHE. The batteries took up an batwry position of 23rd D.A. coming into KEERSELEARE — WINNIPEG section of S. front, in addition the batteries of the 48th D.A. and the 126 N. and 155th A.F.A. Brigades came under command of C.R.A. 58th Division, and were grouped as follows. LEFT GROUP 291-126 CENTRE GROUP Bty 241, RIGHT GROUP 290-155, with the respectively at LA-BELLE ALLIANCE, HILL TOP and WILSON'S FARM. Wagon lines were near VLAMERTINGHE. During this period, continuous harassing fire was kept up on enemy's communications to the LANGEMARCK LINE and	

WAR DIARY or INTELLIGENCE SUMMARY

Army Form C. 2118.

Place	Date	Hour	Summary of Events and Information	Remarks and references to Appendices
YPRES.	7-9-17 to 9-9-17		his posts. Much gun was fired by 4.5" howitzers against known active batteries. Wire-cutting was necessary and conducted. Much successful sniping and anti-personnel Slinger points, also. The Heavy Artillery were bombarding.	
	10-9-17		Barrage fired in support of 1/74th on HUBNER TRENCH.	
	18/9h.		" " " " attack on "16". WINNIPEG, in co-operation with attack by Rt. Flank Division on HILL 35. The 93rd, 298th, and 5th A.F.A. Brigades formed 58th Divisional Artillery Group; Thirsk-Ga were employed as ARMY GROUP with HQ at ENGLISH FARM, and the 5th became PARKER'S GROUP. HQ at HASLAR HOUSE, ST. JEAN. Preliminary bombardment begun.	
	19-9-17. 3a.m.		and occupied duty of barrages and sweeping and searching whole front with bursts of gas fire. HQ moved up to CANAL BANK —	
→ hsent.	13/14 h.		Barrage fired in support of attack by 173 on CEMETERY and WINNIPEG.	

WAR DIARY or INTELLIGENCE SUMMARY

Army Form C. 2118

Place	Date	Hour	Summary of Events and Information	Remarks and references to Appendices
YPRES	20.9.17	5.40 a.m.	The Division attacked the LANGEMARCK LINE from KE opposite KEERZELAERE to OLIVE HOUSE. All objectives were gained except one gun pit about J.1.a.6 central. Creepers, standing and enemy barrages were fired by this Artillery. Group is support of these operations. Our own Infantry had prisoners teeth to the efficiency of our barrage. Subsequent to this attack many S.O.S. calls were answered, and several counter-attacks were broken up and enemy heavy concentrations covered with enemy.	
	21- 25.9.17		During this period, in intensified harassing fire was kept up on the enemy's new front line. Daily barrages were fired also, to prevent him repairing his wire, and annoy him as to our intentions.	
	26.9.17 5.50 a.m.		BARKER'S GROUP were moved on the 15th to area of KITCHENER'S WOOD, and left open zone, the movement LA BELLE ALLIANCE After the hour attack is there bombardment, our infantry	

WAR DIARY
or
INTELLIGENCE SUMMARY.
(Erase heading not required.)

Army Form C. 2118.

Place	Date	Hour	Summary of Events and Information	Remarks and references to Appendices
YPRES.	26.9.17		again attacked. VALE HOUSE AVIATIK FARM and DEAR HOUSE were captured. Many trench-shafts again were blown up by punctual response to S.O.S. signals, in conjunction with L.G. and M.G. fire.	
	26.9.17.		The Division was relieved of Major Division. C.R.A. 47th Division took over from C.R.A. 58th Division at 10 a.m. Period taken over the Brigades of the 58th Division had been relieved by Brigades and 53rd Brigades of 18th Division. Our batteries remained in action; R.A. H.Q. moved into Divisional Headquarters to RECEIVE and were billeted at LANDRETHUM. During this period our batteries have been heavily shelled, and several guns, especially howitzers were landed up. Casualties have fortunately been light. Hostile guns were also consistently active on WIEHAL DYKE and LA BASSÉE areas. Bombing raids against our wagon lines were also reported.	

T2134. Wt. W708-776. 500000. 4/15. Sir J. C. & S.

WAR DIARY or INTELLIGENCE SUMMARY

Army Form C. 2118

OCTOBER, 1917.

Place	Date	Hour	Summary of Events and Information	Remarks and references to Appendices
YPRES			The Brigade of Artillery were in action in the vicinity of SMITH'S Road and KITCHENER'S WOOD during this period. They covered the hostile of the 63rd Division in the operations against the hostile positions 48th, 9th S.E. of POELCAPPELLE and the 14th, 18th, 26th and 30th. The batteries were advanced to positions in the STEENBEEK and along the LANGEMARK — WINNIPEG and POELCAPPELLE — ST. JULIEN roads. The batteries came in for a lot of shelling and counterbattery fire on the part of the enemy, and the stubbornness of the ammunition supply and the appalling state of the ground, made both a matter of great difficulty.	(sgd)
	31-10-17		The Brigadier received the Brigade of the 18th D.A., and in the 16th went to the RECEIVES as they were from the D.A., anomaly the C.R.A. 58th Division was in command of the Artillery covering the POELCAPPELLE sector. H.Q. of C.M.A. in PEAK CAMP.	Miles B.G.R.A. Cmdy 58. B R Artillery

SECRET.

Copy No. 69

58th Divisional Artillery Group Order No. 49.

1. October 28th is Q.(a) day. and a 48 hours' preliminary bombardment of the enemy's positions will commence at 6.30 a.m.

2. This bombardment will be directed against the first 100 - 1200 yards East of our front line - its main object will be the destruction of the hostile garrison of this area.

3. Strong points and likely positions which may be occupied by the hostile troops detailed to hold the front system will be bombarded and barrages will be carried out over the whole area of the front system.
    Also by night a barrage will be put down to isolate the garrison of the front system, and the reserve troops, on a line about 3000 yards from our front line will be harassed.

4. Three barrages will be fired each day and the remainder of the day will be divided into bombardment periods.

5. BARRAGES.

    The following will be the barrages -

    (1) BARRAGE "A".

        All 18-pdrs. and 4.5" Hows. will come down on a line 1200 yards from our front line, and at O plus 2 minutes will creep back by lifts of 50 yards every 2 minutes till the following lines are reached :-

        18-pdrs.   150 yards from our front line.

        4.5" Hows. 250   "   "   "   "

    (2) BARRAGE "B".

        As in Barrage "A", but 18 pdrs. will jump from the 400 yards line to the 150 yards line, dwell 2 minutes, and then creep forward by 50 yard lifts to the 600 yards line, and after dwelling there 2 minutes, will cease fire.

        4.5" Hows. on reaching the 250 yards line, dwell 4 minutes and then cease fire.

    (3) BARRAGE "C".

        At O, 18-pdrs. and 4.5" Hows. will come down on the 150 and 250 yard lines respectively and will lift irregularly backwards and forwards between above lines and the 600 yards line till O plus 16, at which time they will be on the 600 yards line.

2.

At O plus 18 they will creep forward by 50 yard lifts every 2 minutes to the 1200 yards line and then cease fire.

6. Rates of fire for above barrages :-

<u>18-pdrs.</u>   1 round per gun per minute.

<u>4.5" Hows.</u>   ½ round per how. per minute.

Any deficiency, due to guns or hows. being out of action, must be compensated for by increasing the rate of fire.

Barrages should not be of equal strength all along the front, but should be thickened in places according to the tactical and ground conditions.

7. <u>BOMBARDMENTS.</u>

The bombardment of strong points and likely positions for enemy troops will be divided into three periods :-

(1) <u>PERIOD "A".</u>

Bombardment by Heavy Artillery.

18-pdrs. will fire bursts to catch runners, and also on a line 100 yards from our front line.

(2) <u>PERIOD "B".</u>

Bombardment by 18-pdrs. and 4.5" Hows. of enemy's front line and likely places for his support troops between 800 and 1200 yards from our front line.

When weather is favourable, 4.5" Hows. will use gas.

(3) <u>PERIOD "C".</u>   NIGHT TIME.

(a) Harassing fire by Heavies.

(b) Harassing fire by 18-pdrs. and 4.5" Hows.

The following amount of ammunition will be expended by each Group during the bombardment periods.

	DURING "B" PERIOD.	DURING "A" PERIOD.	DURING "C" PERIODS. "C" (b) PERIODS.
18-pdrs. B Group	2700	750	1500
Both C Group	2700	750	1500
days D Group	2700	750	1500
4th D.A. Group	2700	750	1500
57th D.A. Group	2700	750	1500
4.5" Hows. B Group	1200)	NIL	500)
1st Day. C Group	1200)In-	NIL	500)Including
D Group	1200)cluding	NIL	500) Gas.
4th D.A. Group	1200)Gas.	NIL	500)
57th D.A. Group	1200)	NIL	500)
4.5" Hows. B Group	850	NIL	850
2nd Day. C Group	850	NIL	850
D Group	850	NIL	850
4th D.A. Group	850	NIL	850
57th D.A. Group	850	NIL	850

8. TIME TABLE.

FIRST DAY.

6.30 a.m. to 7 a.m.	Period B
7.10 a.m.	Barrage "C"
8 a.m. to 9 a.m.	Period B
9 a.m. to noon	Period A.
Noon to 2 p.m.	Period B.
2 p.m. to 5 p.m.	Period A.
5 p.m. to 6 p.m.	Period B
6 p.m. to 7 p.m.	Period C (b)
7.20 p.m.	Barrage B.
8 p.m. to 10.45 p.m.	Period C (b)
11 p.m.	Barrage A.
End of Barrage A to 5.30 a.m. (2nd Day)	Period C (a)

SECOND DAY.

5.30 a.m. to 8 a.m.	Period B.
8 a.m. to 10 a.m.	Period A.
10.25 a.m.	Barrage B.
End of Barrage B to Noon	Period B.
Noon to 4 p.m.	Period A.
4 p.m. to 5.30 p.m.	Period B.
5.30 p.m. to 8 p.m.	Period C (b)
8.20 p.m.	Barrage A.
End of Barrage A to 11.30 p.m.	Period C (b)
11.50 p.m.	Barrage C.
End of Barrage C to an hour to be notified later	Period C (a)

4.

9. Group lanes for "Barrages" and "bombardments" will be as shewn on attached sketch map.

10. All guns of "B", "C", "D", "4th D.A." and "57th D.A." Groups will fire all barrages.

   With regard to the periods for bombardment, the number of guns to be employed is left to the discretion of Group Commanders, but the total allotment of ammunition must be fired.

   For Period "B" (Bombardments) which has the largest allotment, it may be difficult to get off the ammunition if many guns are kept silent, but, if possible, the most exposed should not fire.

   Period "C" (b) (Harassing) only takes place at dusk and probably exposed batteries could shoot.

   Period "A" (Spattering), the least exposed batteries can carry out.

11. ACKNOWLEDGE.

H.Q.R.A.,
28th October 1917.
N.

Captain,
Brigade Major, R.A.,
58th Divisional Arty. Group.

Copies to :-
	Copy No.
"A" Group	1 - 9
"B" Group	10 - 18
"C" Group	19 - 27
"D" Group	28 - 36
4th D.A. Group	37 - 45
57th D.A. Group	46 - 54
R.A., XVIIth Corps	55
H.A., XVIIIth Corps	56
58th Division "G"	57
57th Divisional Artillery	58
63rd Divisional Artillery	59
32nd Divisional Artillery	60
18th Divisional Artillery	61
173rd Infy. Bde.	62
174th Infy. Bde.	63
175th Infy. Bde.	64
L.O., 174th Infy. Bde.	65
Staff Captain, R.A.	66
R.A., R.A.	67
Signal Officer, R.A.	68
War Diary	69 - 70
File	71 - 72

SECRET.   COPY NO: 49

58TH DIVISIONAL ARTILLERY ORDER NO: 45.

Reference POELCAPPELLE Sheet
1/10,000, Ed. 3.

1. At 10.0 a.m. on October 25th the 58th Division will have relieved the 18th Division and the command of the artillery covering the divisional front passes to the C.R.A., 58th Div.

2. There will be no alteration in the tactical dispositions or zones allotted to the existing groups, with the exception of certain reliefs for which orders have been issued separately.

3. On October 26th, at a zero hour to be notified later, the offensive will be resumed and our troops will establish themselves on the line marked RED on attached map. A pause of about 45 minutes will be made on the dotted RED LINE.

4. The attack will be carried out by the 173rd Infantry Brigade (Brigadier-General R.B. Morgan, D.S.O.) with Headquarters at VARNA FARM, C.4.a.5.3.

   The capture and ten retention of PAPA FARM and the high ground about WHITECHAPEL are of the utmost importance.

5. The 63rd Division are also attacking on our right, and the 57th Division of the XIV Corps on our left. Touch with the former will be obtained by visual across the LEKKERBOTTERBEEK and with the latter at SPIDER CROSS ROADS.

6. Liaison duties will be performed as follows -

   With Brigadier General   Major E.Conolly,R.F.A.
   Command 173rd Infantry
   Brigade - VARNA Farm

   With Headquarters of attack-   A Captain to be detailed
   ing Battalions - V.19.a.6.1.   by O.C. "A" Group.

7. O.Ps. will be manned as usual and, in addition, F.O.Os. will be provided as follows, who must endeavour to occupy position from which the ground immediately in front of the objective can be seen -

   A. Group.   1 F.O.O. in neighbourhood of
                   OXFORD HOUSE.

   B.& C.Groups. 1 F.O.O. each in neighbourhood of
                   MEUNIER HOUSE.

   D. Group   1 F.O.O. in neighbourhood of
                   STRING House.

- 2 -

Those detailed by "B" & "C" Groups will be provided with rifles and the necessary rifle grenades for repeating the S.O.S. signal back to batteries when sent up.

Every effort to maintain communications, both by runner and visual, must be made and parties organised as in S.S.148.

8. All units of the 58th Divisional Artillery Group will cover the attack.

The localities on which fire is to be brought to bear, and the times of lifts, are shewn on map issued herewith.

The lanes allotted to Groups are also shewn.

9. The Creeping Barrage will open at zero on a line 150 yards beyond the forming up place of our infantry and remain for 8 minutes after which it creeps 50 yards and continues doing so every 4 minutes, till it rests on those lines shown for protective barrage conforming to the time shown on the map. 75% of the available 18-prs: in each Group will be used for this purpose, and the fire of batteries superimposed on one another in each brigade.

10. The combining barrage will search and sweep the ground between 150 yards and 400 yards beyond the creeper. 25% of the available 18-prs: and all available 4.5" hows: will be used for this purpose.

Care must be taken that fire is concentrated on those parts of the terrain which are not shewn as waterlogged in aerial photographs.

Group Commanders will also arrange that all known strong points are kept under fire from at least 1 18-pr: and 1 4.5" how: throughout the extreme time for which they remain within the limits of the combing barrage. For this case, 18-prs: will use H.E. and for the last 8 minutes before it is time that these individual guns should lift, their rate of fire will be quickened to 4 and 3 rounds per gun per minute respectively.

Special attention must be paid by O.C. "B" Group to CAMERON HOUSE, and in this case the fire of 2 18-prs: and 2 4.5" hows: must be kept on the centre of this pocket until the creeper lifts at 0.48.

11. The protective barrage will consist of shrapnel except for strong points, against which H.E. will be used by the 18-prs:

In both 1st and 2nd protective barrages, as soon as a rate of 1 round per gun per minute has been reached, the fire will be by salvoes, fired over at least a Brigade front, and searching within a limit of 400 yards beyond it.

-3-

Group Commanders will issue time table detailing the times at which these salvoes must be fired, and every available gun will be employed to avoid gaps through which the enemy might pass his troops.

12. 50% of the 18-prs: and all the 4.5" hows: of "D" Group will cease firing at 1.40, and switch so as to distribute their fire by reinforcing comb: ing barrage over the whole divisional front South of V.15.central. They will re-open fire on those lines at 1.56 and continue on them till 2.30 when they will resume their original tasks on their own Group front.

13. RATES OF FIRE.

	Rounds per gun per min.	
	18-prs:	4.5" hows:

Creeping Barrage.

0.0 - 0.8	4.	3.
0.8 - End of Creeper	3.	2.

Comb. ing Barrage.

As for Creeping Barrage till final Protector is reached, then as for Protector

Protective Barrage.

1st half hour of each Protective Barrage	2.	1.
Remainder of Protective Barrage	1.	½.
except for last 8 minutes of 1st Protective Barrage, when, in order to signal to the infantry to advance, it will be	3.	2.

Correctors will be calculated so that 25% of the shrapnel fired burst on graze.

14. Smoke barrages will be fired as under -

A.Group. 4 18-prs: taken from the comb. ing barrage will fire smoke immediately in front of PAPA Farm and 100 yards South of it, so as to screen CAMERON House, from 0.32 - 0.60.

D.Group. 4 18-prs: taken from the comb: ing barrage will fire smoke between V.15.c.30.95. - V.15.a.20.20. from 0.35 - 0.40.

Rate of fire for smoke barrages will be 4 rounds per gun per minute for first 2 minutes, after that, 1 round per gun per minute.

-4-

All guns, on completion of these smoke barrages, will return to their normal tasks in the combining barrages.

No smoke shell will be fired unless the wind blows between W. and S.W.

15. A counter attack plane will be up continuously throughout day light from zero onwards, to detect the approach of hostile counter attack. When this patrol observes a hostile party of 100 or more moving to a counter attack, it will drop a smoke bomb over that portion of the front towards which they are moving.

The bomb will burst about 100 feet below the plane into a white parachute light which descends slowly, leaving a long trail of brown smoke about one foot broad behind it.

16. On completion of the operation the S.O.S. Line will be that of the final protective barrage, pending further orders on the subject.

17. Watches will be synchronised at Group Headquarters, CANE POST, where a watch will be sent with the correct time from R.A. Headquarters at 4.30 p.m. on October 25th.

No synchronisation will be done over the telephone.

18. ACKNOWLEDGE.

H. Williamson
Captain
Brigade Major, R.A.,
58th Divisional Arty.

24th October, 1917.

DISTRIBUTION -

A. Group.	1 - 9.
B. Group.	10 - 18.
C. Group.	19 - 27.
D. Group.	28 - 37.
XVIII Corps, R.A.	38.
XVIII Corps, H.A.	39.
58th Division 'G'.	40.
57th Div'nl Artillery	41.
63rd Div'nl Artillery	42.
32nd Div'nl Artillery	43.
18th Div'nl Artillery	44.
173rd Inf. Brigade	45.
L.O. 173rd Inf. Bde.	46.
Staff Captain	47.
Reconnaissance Officer	48.
War Diary	49 - 50.
File	51 - 52.

SECRET

XVIII Corps No. G.S.66/21/34

58th Divisional Artillery Group.(confirming telephone message)
58th Division.
63rd Divisional Artillery Group.("   "   "   )
63rd Division.
7th Squadron R.F.C.
XVIII Corps Heavy Artillery.

The Bombardment carried out on "N" day will be repeated on "Q(a)" day, except that the "A" barrage at 11 p.m. will not be fired.

Ammunition expenditure as on "N" day.

58th and 63rd Divisions will send lists of points they wish bombarded to G.O.C., H.A., and to this Office at once.

Q(a) Period will commence at 11 p.m.

H.J. Amos Capt
General Staff, XVIII Corps.

27/10/17.

Copies to :-

R.A. Fifth Army.
XVIII Corps "Q"
M.G.O., XVIII Corps.
Counter Battery Staff Officer.
R.A. XIV Corps.
R.A. Canadian Corps.
15th Wing R.F.C.
Staff Captain R.A., XVIII Corps.

14e/7.6
14e/7.3
2a k 7.8
2b l 5.6
2c h 4.3
2d d 5.0
Traca

SECRET. Copy No. ....

58th Divisional Artillery Group Order No. 51.

Reference Sheet.   POELCAPPELLE   1/10,000   Edtn 3.

1. On October 30th at a ZERO Hour to be notified later, the 58th Division will resume its attack on the hostile positions and establish itself on the objective marked on attached Barrage Map.

2. The attack will be carried out by the 2/8th Battn. London Regt. of the 174th Infantry Brigade.
   The 63rd R.N. Division will also be attacking on the Right flank.

3. The attack will be covered by B, C, D, 4th D.A., and 57th D.A. Groups, which comprise the whole 58th Divisional Artillery Group.

4. Liaison will be performed with 174th Infantry Brigade H.Q. at VARNA FARM by Lt. Col. Stillwell, 83rd Army Bde. R.F.A. and C Group will detail a captain or senior subaltern to act as Liaison Officer with H.Q., 2/8th Battn. London Regiment (Lt.Col. Dervych Jones, D.S.O., M.C.) at V.19.a.7.1.
   These officers will report as above by 3 p.m. October 29th.

5. O.P.s will be manned as usual but each Group will send forward one F.O.O. with a suitable party to establish themselves on ground from which they can see the part of the objective on to which their Group fires.   Those going to MEUNIER HOUSE will provide themselves with a rifle and S.O.S. rifle grenades with which to pass on an S.O.S. from the front if necessary.   These can be obtained through Staff Captain, 174th Infantry Brigade.

6. Instructions for communications are issued separately.

7. The CREEPING BARRAGE will come down at ZERO on a line 150^X in front of our Infantry's forming-up place as shewn on attached Barrage Map.
   It will remain 8 minutes and then creep forward as shewn at the rate of 50^X in 6 minutes.
   A pause of 30 minutes will be made on the dotted line.
   75% of the available 18 pounders in each Group will be used for this purpose and the fire of each battery superimposed in each Brigade.

8. The COMBING BARRAGE will search and sweep the ground from 150 to 400 yards beyond the CREEPING BARRAGE and throughout the PROTECTIVE BARRAGE.
   25% of the available 18 pounder batteries and all available 4.5" How. Batteries will be used for this purpose.
   Care must be taken not to waste shell on parts of the ground which are waterlogged.
   Group Commanders will also arrange that 1 - 18 pdr. and 1 - 4.5" How. will be kept on each strong point on their Group front throughout the period for which it remains within the limits of the COMBING BARRAGE except in the case of the 18 pdr. which will not leave these strong points until joined by the CREEPING BARRAGE. For this purpose 18 pdrs. will use H.E. and for the last 8 minutes before it is time for these individual guns to lift off the strong points, the rate of fire will be quickened to 4 rounds per gun and 3 rounds per Howitzer per minute.

9. The /

9. The PROTECTIVE BARRAGES will consist of shrapnel except for those guns detailed to fire on strong points.
After a rate of 1 round per gun per minute has been reached by each PROTECTIVE BARRAGE, fire will be by salvoes over at least a brigade front at a time. The ground up to a limit of 400^X beyond the PROTECTIVE BARRAGE being thoroughly searched.
Group Commanders will issue time table detailing the times at which these salvoes must be fired, and every available gun will be employed to avoid gaps through which the enemy might pass his troops.

10. Smoke barrages will be fired as under.

   B Group will detail 4 - 18 pounder guns from the COMBING BARRAGE to fire smoke on a line 100^X each side of V.15.c.5.1. on the line of the FINAL PROTECTIVE BARRAGE from 0.0 - 1.10.

   C Group will detail 4 - 4.5" Hows. to fire smoke 100^X N. and S. of V.16.c.2.6. (Cross Roads) from 0.0 - 2.0.

   All guns, on completion of these smoke barrages, will return to their normal tasks in the COMBING BARRAGES.

   No smoke shell will be fired unless the wind blows between W. and S.W.

11. A special Barrage will be fired by 1 - 18 pdr. battery each from C and D Groups.
They will search the SRRIET ROAD and cover ground 200^X each side of it with irregular bursts of searching fire.
100 rounds per battery will be fired each hour from the time of arrival at FINAL PROTECTIVE BARRAGE till 1 hour after dawn on October 31st.
These Batteries may be relieved of their tasks by other batteries under Group arrangements.
All shrapnel will be used.

12. RATES OF FIRE.

	Rounds per gun per min.	
	18 pdrs.	4.5" Hows.
CREEPING BARRAGE.		
0.0 - 0.8	4	3
0.8 - End of Creeper	3	2
COMBING BARRAGE.		
As for CREEPING BARRAGE till FINAL PROTECTOR is reached, then as for PROTECTOR.		
PROTECTIVE BARRAGE.		
1st half hour of each PROTECTIVE BARRAGE	2	1
Remainder of PROTECTIVE BARRAGE	1	½
except for last 8 minutes of 1st PROTECTIVE BARRAGE, when, in order to signal to the infantry to advance, it will be	3	2

All correctors will be calculated so that 25% of the shrapnel fired burst on graze.

SMOKE BARRAGE.

9. Group lanes for "Barrages" and "bombardments" will be as shewn on attached sketch map.

10. All guns of "B", "C", "D", "4th D.A." and "57th D.A." Groups will fire all barrages.

    With regard to the periods for bombardment, the number of guns to be employed is left to the discretion of Group Commanders, but the total allotment of ammunition must be fired.

    For Period "B" (Bombardments) which has the largest allotment, it may be difficult to get off the ammunition if many guns are kept silent, but, if possible, the most exposed should not fire.

    Period "C" (b) (Harassing) only takes place at dusk and probably exposed batteries could shoot.

    Period "A" (Spattering), the least exposed batteries can carry out.

11. ACKNOWLEDGE.

H.Q.R.A.,
28th October 1917.
N.

Captain,
Brigade Major, R.A.,
58th Divisional Arty. Group.

Copies to :-	Copy No.
"A" Group	1 - 9
"B" Group	10 - 18
"C" Group	19 - 27
"D" Group	28 - 36
4th D.A. Group	37 - 45
57th D.A. Group	46 - 54
R.A., XVIIth Corps	55
H.A., XVIIIth Corps	56
58th Division "G"	57
57th Divisional Artillery	58
63rd Divisional Artillery	59
32nd Divisional Artillery	60
18th Divisional Artillery	61
173rd Infy. Bde.	62
174th Infy. Bde.	63
175th Infy. Bde.	64
L.O., 174th Infy. Bde.	65
Staff Captain, R.A.	66
R.O., R.A.	67
Signal Officer, R.A.	68
War Diary	69 - 70
File	71 - 72.

		DURING "B" PERIOD.	DURING "A" PERIOD.	DURING "C" PERIODS. "C" (b) PERIODS.
18-pdrs. Both days	B Group C Group D Group 4th D.A. Group 57th D.A. Group	2700 2700 2700 2700 2700	750 750 750 750 750	1500 1500 1500 1500 1500
4.5" Hows. 1st Day.	B Group C Group D Group 4th D.A. Group 57th D.A. Group	1200) 1200)In- 1200)clud-)ing 1200)Gas.) 1200)	NIL NIL NIL NIL NIL	500) 500)Includ- 500) ing) Gas. 500)) 500)
4.5" Hows. 2nd Day.	B Group C Group D Group 4th D.A. Group 57th D.A. Group	850 850 850 850 850	NIL NIL NIL NIL NIL	850 850 850 850 850

8. TIME TABLE.

FIRST DAY.

6.30 a.m. to 7 a.m.	Period B
7.10 a.m.	Barrage "C"
8 a.m. to 9 a.m.	Period B
9 a.m. to noon	Period A.
Noon to 2 p.m.	Period B.
2 p.m. to 5 p.m.	Period A.
5 p.m. to 6 p.m.	Period B
6 p.m. to 7 p.m.	Period C (b)
7.20 p.m.	Barrage B.
8 p.m. to 10.45 p.m.	Period C (b)
11 p.m.	Barrage A.
End of Barrage A to 5.30 a.m. (2nd Day)	Period C (a)

SECOND DAY.

5.30 a.m. to 8 a.m.	Period B.
8 a.m. to 10 a.m.	Period A.
10.25 a.m.	Barrage B.
End of Barrage B to Noon	Period B.
Noon to 4 p.m.	Period A.
4 p.m. to 5.30 p.m.	Period B.
5.30 p.m. to 8 p.m.	Period C (b)
8.20 p.m.	Barrage A.
End of Barrage A to 11.30 p.m.	Period C (b)
11.50 p.m.	Barrage C.
End of Barrage C to an hour to be notified later	Period C (a)

SECRET.

Copy No. 52

58th Divisional Artillery Group Order No. 55.

1. Tomorrow, November 4th, is X (a) and a bombardment of the enemy's positions will take place. It will consist of
   (a) An Army Barrage as detailed in Barrage Table "A" attached.
       ZERO Hour 4.40 a.m.

   (b) Bursts of fire on selected points as detailed in Table "B" attached which will be fired in accordance with the following time-table :-

6.15 p.m. - 6.45 p.m.	Silent period.
6.45 p.m. - 6.51 p.m.	Burst of fire.
7.20 p.m. - 7.35 p.m.	Silent period.
8.00 p.m. - 8.20 p.m.	Silent period.
8.20 p.m. - 8.26 p.m.	Burst of fire.

   During Silent periods NO Gun or Howitzer on 58th Divisional Artillery Group Front will fire, so as to enable the Sound Ranging Section to function.

2. Rates of fire for (a) and (b)
18 - pounders	2 rounds per gun per min.
4.5" Hows.	1 round per gun per min.

   Nature of shell (a) 50% Shrapnel and H.E. for 18-pdrs.
                     (b) All H.E.

3. In the Army Barrage detailed in para. 1 (a) all lifts will be within the zones at present covered by the respective Groups.

4. ACKNOWLEDGE.

H Williamson
Captain,
Brigade Major, R.A.,
58th Divisional Artillery Group.

H.Q.R.A.,
3rd November 1917.
N.

Distribution :-   Copies No.
A Group	1 - 9
B Group	10 - 18
C Group	19 - 27
D Group	28 - 36
R.A. II Corps	37
H.A. II Corps	38
58th Division "G"	39
57th Div. Arty.	40
63rd Div. Arty.	41
32nd Div. Arty.	42
18th Div. Arty.	43
175th Infy. Bde.	44
Liaison Officer, 175th In Bde.	45
173rd Infy. Bde.	46
174th Infy. Bde.	47
Staff Captain, R.A.	48
R.O.R.A.	49
Signal Officer R.A.	50
War Diary	51 - 52
File	53 - 54

BARRAGE TABLE.

Table "A"

1. 0.0   2/3 of available 18-pdrs. in each Group open on their S.O.S.
             Lines and remain   till 0.3
    0.3   Lift 100x   and remain   till 0.6
    0.6   Lift 100x   and remain   till 0.9
    0.9   Lift 100x   and remain   till 0.12
    0.12   Lift 100x   and remain   till 0.18
    0.18   Drop 100x   and remain   till 0.21
    0.21   Drop 100x   and remain   till 0.24
    0.24   STOP   0.27
    0.27   Lift 400x   and remain   till 0.30
    0.30   Drop 600x   and remain   till 0.33
    0.33   STOP

2. 0.0   1/3 of available 18-pdrs. open on a line 100x beyond their
             S.O.S. Line
    0.3   Lift 100x   and remain   till 0.6
    0.6   Lift 100x   and remain   till 0.9
    0.9   Lift 100x   and remain   till 0.12
    0.12   Lift 100x   and remain   till 0.15
    0.15   Lift 100x   and remain   till 0.18
    0.18   Drop 100x   and remain   till 0.21
    0.21   Drop 100x   and remain   till 0.24
    0.24   STOP FIRING   0.27
    0.27   Lift 300x   and remain   till 0.30
    0.30   Drop 500x   and remain   till 0.33
    0.33   STOP

3. 0.0   All available 4.5" Hows. open on a line 100x yards beyond the
             18-pdr. S.O.S. Lines and remain   till 0.3
    0.3   Lift 100x   and remain   till 0.6
    0.6   Lift 100x   and remain   till 0.9
    0.9   Lift 100x   and remain   till 0.12
    0.12   Lift 100x   and remain   till 0.18
    0.18   Drop 100x   and remain   till 0.21
    0.21   Drop /

3 Contd.

0.21	Drop 100ˣ
0.24	STOP FIRING
0.27	Lift 400ˣ
0.33	Drop 300ˣ
0.36	STOP

and remain till 0.24
and remain till 0.27
and remain till 0.33
and remain till 0.36

TABLE "B".

GROUP	First Burst of fire 6.45 p.m. - 6.51 p.m.	Second Burst of fire 8.20 p.m. - 8.26 p.m.
A	Huts and buildings at V.16.c.6.3	CLEAR FARM
B	Huts and buildings at V.16.c.6.3.	CLEAR FARM
C	Road from T in SPRIET - V.16.d.50.75	Concrete pill boxes in V.16.b.10.59
D	Roads from T in SPRIET - V.16.d.50.75	Point V.16.a.55.95

WAR DIARY

HQ, R.A. ~~INTELLIGENCE SUMMARY~~
58th Division

Army Form C. 2118.

Nov: 1917

Place	Date	Hour	Summary of Events and Information	Remarks and references to Appendices
YPRES	31/10/17 -1/11/17		Batteries of this Divisional Artillery were relieved in action by the batteries of the 1st D.A. R.A., H.Q. remained. G.O.C., R.A. the G.O.C., R.A. 58th Division having command of the left Divisional Artillery Group of 11 Corps.	Pa.
	2.m.m.		Brigades and D.A.C. marched to WORMHOUDT area, staging for RECQUES area.	Pa.
	12/3M		The Divisional Artillery moved down to SAMER area.	Pa.
			H.Q. R.A. FRENCQ, 290 NOIRCARREL 291 ATTIN, 340 LONGVILLERS MARESVILLE 7M. G.O.C., R.A. relieved the G.O.C., R.A. 18th Division in command of the Divisional Artillery of FRENCQ.	Pa.
	17 "			Pa.
	15 "		R.A. Headquarters moved to LEFAUX. During this period rest & refitting, Training has been carried out and Battery training commenced.	Pa.

M.M.Peake
B.G.
C.R.A. 58th Division

R.a.
R.a.
B.S.D.L....

SECRET.   Copy No. 52

58th Divisional Artillery Group Order No. 56.

1.   Tomorrow November 5th is "Y" (a) day and the preliminary bombardment will be continued as follows:-

(a)   An Army barrage as detailed in Barrage Table "A"

            Zero hour................5.40 a.m.

(b)   Bursts of fire on selected points as detailed in Table "B" and in accordance with the following Time Table:-

    6.20 p.m. - 6.40 p.m.   Silent Period.
    7.40 p.m. - 7.46 p.m.   Burst of fire.
    8.20 p.m. - 8.50 p.m.   Silent Period.
    8.50 p.m. - 8.56 p.m.   Burst of fire.

2.   Rates of fire for (a) and (b)
            18 pounders   2 rounds per gun per minute.
            4.5" Hows.   1 round per gun per minute.

        Nature of shell for 18 pounders
            (a) 50% H.E. and Shrapnel.
            (b) All H.E.

        During Silent periods NO gun or howitzer on the 58th Divisional Artillery Group front will fire so as to enable the Sound Ranging Section to function.

3.   All lifts detailed in Barrage Table "A" will be within the limits of the zones at present covered by the respective Groups.

4.   ACKNOWLEDGE.

H.Q.R.A.   Captain,
4/11/17.   Brigade Major, R.A.
T.2.   58th Divisional Artillery Group.

Copies to all recipients of 58th D.A.Group Order No.55.

BARRAGE TABLE "A".

1. 0.0   2/3 of the 18-pounders in each Group open fire on their
          S.O.S. Line

   0.3   Lift 100ˣ   and remain till 0.5
   0.6   Lift 100ˣ   and remain till 0.9
   0.9   Lift 100ˣ   and remain till 0.12
   0.12   Drop 300ˣ   and remain till 0.18
   0.18   Lift 500ˣ   and remain till 0.21
   0.21   Lift 100ˣ   and remain till 0.24
   0.24   Lift 100ˣ   and remain till 0.27
   0.27   Drop 400ˣ   and remain till 0.30
   0.30   STOP

2. 0.0   1/3 of the 18-pounders in each Group open on a line 100ˣ
          beyond our S.O.S. Line and

   0.3   Lift 100ˣ   and remain till 0.6
   0.6   Lift 100ˣ   and remain till 0.9
   0.9   Lift 100ˣ   and remain till 0.12
   0.12   Drop 200ˣ   and remain till 0.18
   0.18   Lift 500ˣ   and remain till 0.21
   0.21   Lift 100ˣ   and remain till 0.24
   0.24   Lift 100ˣ   and remain till 0.27
   0.27   Drop 600ˣ   and remain till 0.30
   0.30   STOP

3. 0.0   All 4.5" Hows. open on a line 100ˣ beyond the 18-pdr. S.O.S.
          Line and

   0.3   Lift 100ˣ   and remain till 0.6
   0.6   Lift 100ˣ   and remain till 0.9
   0.9   Drop 100ˣ   and remain till 0.12
   0.12   Drop 100ˣ   and remain till 0.18
   0.18   Lift 300ˣ   and remain till 0.21
   0.21   Lift 100ˣ   and remain till 0.24
   0.24   Lift 100ˣ   and remain till 0.27
   0.27   Drop 400ˣ   and remain till 0.30
   0.30   STOP

T A B L E "B".

Reference Map. - Tracing of Communications and approaches issued for harassing fire 30.10.17.

Group	First Burst of fire 7.40 p.m. - 7.46 p.m.	Second Burst of Fire 8.50 p.m. - 8.56 p.m.
A	S. track leading to HINTON FARM	N. track leading to HINTON FARM.
B	Track leading to PAPA FARM Howitzers on Sunken Road V.21.a.	Track leading to CAMERON HOUSE as far as SPRIET Road, Howitzers on Sunken Road V.21.a.
C	SPRIET ROAD from V.15.c.5.2 - V.15.d.0.3	Track from V.15.c.6.5. - V.15.d.5.9.
D	Track passing through V.15.central	Tracks V.15.b.3.6. - V.15.a.8.5.

Unless otherwise detailed Howitzers will fire on the same targets as the 18-pounders and will use 106 fuze when available.

SECRET.   Copy No. 52

58th Divisional Artillery Order No. 57.

1. The Canadian Corps are attacking the enemy's position in front of PASSCHENDAELE to-morrow Z (a) day.

2. The 58th Divisional Artillery Group are co-operating by
(a) A Creeping Barrage as detailed in Barrage Table "A"
(b) Firing a smoke barrage from 0.45 till 2.0 on the line V.29.a.00.50 - V.30.a.40.80.

3. O.C. A Group will detail 20 - 18 pounders to fire the Smoke Barrage detailed in paragraph 2 (b) and draw immediately the necessary ammunition from ZOUAVE DUMP. Approximately 2000 rounds will be required.
   In the event of the wind not being E. or N.E. 50% Shrapnel and H.E. will be fired instead.

4. Rates of fire

	18-pdrs.	4.5" Hows.
	Rounds per gun per min.	
CREEPING BARRAGE	2	1
SMOKE BARRAGE	4 for first 3 mins.	—
then	1 till end.	

5. Natures of ammunition -

   18-pdr.   75% Shrapnel

   4.5" Hows. 106 fuzes as available.

6. Silent periods will be observed on "Z (a)" day as follows

   7.10 p.m. - 7.40 p.m.
   7.46 p.m. - 8.0 p.m.
   8.30 p.m. - 9.0 p.m.

7. Watches will be synchronised with a watch which will be sent to H.Q. "D" Group GOURNIER HUT about C.9.d.5.0. at 5.30 p.m.

8. ZERO hour is 6.0 a.m.

9. ACKNOWLEDGE.

                                        H. Williamson
                                        Captain,
                                        Brigade Major, R.A.,
5th November 1917.   58th Divisional Arty. Group.

   Distribution as for 58th D.A.G. Orders 55 and 56.

BARRAGE TABLE "A".

1. 0.0 2/3 available 18-pounders open on their S.O.S.
          Lines   and remain till 0.3
   0.3 Lift 100^x and remain till 0.6
   0.6 Lift 100^x and remain till 0.9
   0.9 Lift 100^x and remain till 0.12
   0.12 Lift 100^x and remain till 0.15
   0.15 Lift 100^x and remain till 0.18
   0.18 Lift 100^x and remain till 0.21
   0.21 Lift 100^x and remain till 0.30
   0.30 Drop 100^x and remain till 0.39
   0.39 Lift 100^x and remain till 0.45
   0.45 STOP

2. 0.0 1/3 available 18-pounders and all available 4.5"
          Howitzers open on a line 100^x beyond the 18-pounder
          S.O.S. Line and then conform exactly to the lifts
          etc. detailed in para. 1   till   0.45
   0.45 STOP

SECRET.   Copy No. 52

58th Divisional Artillery Group Order No. 58.

1. On "A" day, November 7th., a barrage will be fired as follows :-

   (a) 0.0   2/3 available 18-pdrs. open on their
              S.O.S. Lines   and remain till 0.6
       0.6   Lift 100^X and remain till 0.9
       0.9   Lift 100^X and continue doing so every 3
              minutes   till 0.27
       0.27   Drop 700^X on to S.O.S. Line and remain   till 0.30
       0.30   STOP

   (b) 0.0   1/3 available 18-pdrs open on a line 100^X
              beyond their S.O.S. Line   and remain till 0.6
       0.6   Lift 100^X and conform to the movement of (a)   till 0.27
       0.27   Drop 600^X and remain till   0.30
       0.30   STOP.

   (c) 0.0   All available 4.5" Howitzers open on a line
              100^X beyond the 18-pdr. S.O.S. Line and remain
                                                                      till 0.6
       0.6   Lift 100^X and conform to the movement of (a) and
              (b)   till 0.27
       0.27   Drop 400^X and remain till 0.30
       0.30   STOP

2. Nature of Ammunition -

       18 pounders   50% Shrapnel and H.E.

       4.5" Howitzers   106 fuzes as available.

   Rates of fire -

       18 pounders   2 rounds per gun per minute.
       4.5" Howitzers   1 round per gun per minute.

3. ZERO Hour will be 5.30 a.m.

4. ACKNOWLEDGE.

                                                H. Williamson
                                                       Captain,
                                              Brigade Major, R.A.,
5th November 1917.   58th Divisional Artillery Group.

   Distribution as for 58th D.A.G. Orders 55, 56, and 57.

SECRET.   Copy No. 51

58th Divisional Artillery Group Order No. 59.

1. A practice barrage will be fired on November 7th by the whole of the 58th Divisional Artillery Group.
   Times of lifts and lines upon which fire is to be brought to bear by the respective Groups are shewn on attached Tracing.

2. At ZERO, 2/3 of the available 18-pdrs. open fire on line A.
   1/3 of the available 18-pdrs. open fire on line B.
   All available 4.5" Howitzers open fire on line C.
   On arrival on line E all natures remain till 0.15 then STOP.

   Lifts will be every 3 minutes.
   Times of lifting of 2/3 of 18-pdrs. are shewn on the Tracing; other natures conform.

   Rates of fire - 3 rounds per gun and 2 rounds per How. per minute.
   50% Shrapnel and H.E. will be used, except on line C when all H.E. will be fired.

3. The advance is through 600^x only which can probably be covered by most batteries without moving the trail.
   It may, however, be necessary to call upon the batteries to support a longer advance; it is therefore desirable that they should practise moving the trail in the middle of a Creeping Barrage. When this is done it must be arranged that only 2 guns per battery are in process of moving the trail at a time, and that the remaining 4 guns increase their rate of fire to 4 rounds per gun per minute.
   If this is not done, the volume of fire will be unduly diminished while guns are being switched.
   This also applies to 4.5" Hows. who will increase their rate of fire from 2 to 3 rounds per How. per minute.

4. Observing Officers from each Group will render a report on the depth of the barrage as it appears to them in enfilade. This report, with anything else of interest connected with the barrage, will be rendered by Group Commanders to R.A.H.Q.

5. ZERO Hour will be 1 p.m.

6. ACKNOWLEDGE.

                                              Captain,
                                        Brigade Major, R.A.,
6th November 1917.   58th Divisional Arty. Group.

   Distribution as in 58th D.A.G. Order No. 55.

SECRET.

AMENDMENT to 58th D.A. Group Order No. 59.

Para. 2.   Cancel line 4.

At end of line 7, add -
"maintaining the relative distance until 0.15,
when all STOP."

Cancel last two lines of paragraph and substitute -
"Correctors will be calculated to give 50% on graze.
18-pounders will use shrapnel only except from
0.6 - 0.9 when all natures will use H.E."

ACKNOWLEDGE.

5th November 1917.

Captain,
Brigade Major, R.A.,
58th Divisional Arty. Group.

WD

SECRET.   Copy No. ...52...

58th Divisional Artillery Group Order No. 60.

1. The following preparatory Barrages will be fired on "B" day :-

    (a) A Corps Barrage as detailed in Barrage Table A.1.

        ZERO Hour   4.45 a.m.

    (b) An Army Barrage as detailed in Barrage Table A.2.

        ZERO Hour   6.00 a.m.

    (c) Bursts of fire as detailed in Table B.

2. Silent periods will be maintained from

        6.30 p.m. - 7.00 p.m.
        7.50 p.m. - 8.10 p.m.

3. Rates of fire.   Normal.

   Nature of Ammunition   50% H.E. and Shrapnel.

4. ACKNOWLEDGE.

H. Williamson
                                                Captain,
                                        Brigade Major, R.A.,
6th November 1917.   58th Divisional Arty. Group.

   Distribution as in 58th D.A.G. Order No. 55.

Issued with 5 & D.A.G.O. 40

BARRAGE TABLE A 1.

(a)
0.0	2/3 available 18-pdrs. open on their S.O.S. Lines and remain till	0.3
0.3	Lift 100ˣ and remain till	0.6
0.6	Lift 100ˣ and remain till	0.9
0.9	Lift 100ˣ and remain till	0.12
0.12	Lift 100ˣ and remain till	0.15
0.15	Lift 100ˣ and remain till	0.24
0.24	Drop 100ˣ and remain till	0.27
0.27	Drop 100ˣ and remain till	0.30
0.30	STOP	

(b)
0.0	1/3 available 18-pdrs. and all available 4.5" Howitzers open on a line 100ˣ beyond the 18-pdr. S.O.S. Line and remain till	0.3
0.3	Lift 100ˣ and continue conforming to and keeping 100ˣ ahead of the barrage in 1 (a) till	0.30
0.30	STOP	

Issued with 58 D.A.G.O. 60.

BARRAGE TABLE A 2.

(a)
0.0	2/3 available 18-pdrs. open on their S.O.S. Lines and remain till	0.6
0.6	Lift 200ˣ and remain till	0.9
0.9	Lift 100ˣ and continue lifting 100ˣ every 3 minutes till	0.27
0.27	STOP FIRING till	0.30
0.30	Drop 700ˣ and remain till	0.33
0.33	STOP	

(b)
0.0	1/3 of the available 18-pdrs. open 100ˣ beyond their S.O.S. Lines and remain till	0.6
0.6	Lift 200ˣ and remain till	0.9
0.9	Lift 100 and continue doing so every 3 minutes till	0.27
0.27	STOP FIRING till	0.30
0.30	Drop 600ˣ and remain till	0.33
0.33	STOP	

(c)
0.0	All available 4.5" Howitzers open on a line 100ˣ beyond the 18-pdr. S.O.S. Line and remain till	0.6
0.6	Lift 200ˣ and remain till	0.9
0.9	Lift 100ˣ and continue lifting 100ˣ every 3 minutes till	0.27
0.27	STOP FIRING till	0.30
0.30	Lift 300ˣ and remain till	0.33
0.33	STOP.	

TABLE "B".

Issued with 58th D.A. Group Order No. 60.

Reference Map - Tracing of Communications and approach issued for harassing fire 30/10/17.

Group.	First Burst of fire 7.00 p.m. - 7.6 p.m.	Second Burst of Fire 8.10 p.m. - 8.16 p.m.
A	S. Track leading to HINTON FARM	N. Track leading to HINTON FARM.
B	Track leading to PAPA FARM. Howitzers on Sunken Road V.21.a.	Track leading to CAMERON HOUSE as far as SPRIET Road. Howitzers on Sunken Road in V.21.a.
C	SPRIET ROAD from V.15.c.6.2. - V.15.d.0.3	Track from V.15.c.6.5. - V.15.d.5.9.
D	Track passing through V.15.central	Tracks V.15.b.3.6. - V.15.a.8.5.

Unless otherwise detailed Howitzers will fire on the same targets as the 18-pounders and will use 106 fuze as available.

SECRET.   Copy No. 18

58th Divisional Artillery Group Order No. 61.

1. The following extracts from II Corps R.A. Instruction No. 2 are circulated herewith :-

    (i) Until further notice, orders for preparatory Barrages will be issued by means of Barrage Diagrams (specimen attached)

    (ii) Barrages will be known as

    "A" consisting of 2/3 of the available 18-pounders.

    "B" consisting of 1/3 of the available 18-pounders and all 4.5" Howitzers.

    (iii) The vertical line marked "START" is the normal 18-pdr. S.O.S. Line

    (iv) The horizontal bars above any nature denote the time that nature of gun ceases to fire.

    (v) The normal rates of fire for ARMY Barrages are as follows:-

    18-pounders   2 rounds per gun per minute.

    4.5" How.   1 round per How. per minute.

    (vi) The rates of fire for CORPS Barrages will be ordered as required.

    (vii) **Burst of Fire.**

    The whole area ordered will be covered as far as possible by all natures of artillery and no dividing line between Heavy and Field Artillery will be made. As high a rate as possible will be ordered. Actual objectives will be selected by the C.R.A.

    (viii) During silent periods all guns and howitzers will stop firing to allow the Sound Rangers to function.

2. Attention is drawn to the terms employed in above extracts as they will be used in all orders emanating from this Office, and should a sufficient supply of diagrams be available, they also may be used in detailing preparatory barrages to Group H.Q.

3. ACKNOWLEDGE.

                                           H. Williamson
                                           Captain,
                                           Brigade Major, R.A.,
6th November 1917.   58th Divisional Arty. Group.

Copies to
  All Groups   173rd Infy. Bde.   Liaison Offr. 175th
  R.A. II Corps   174th Infy. Bde.   Infy. Bde.
  58th Division "G" 175th Infy. Bde.   Staff Captain, R.A.

SECRET.   Copy No. ...54...

58th Divisional Artillery Group Order No. 62.

1. The offensive will be resumed by the 1st (Imperial) Division on our Right at an early date.

2. The 58th Divisional Artillery Group will co-operate by forming an Enfilade Creeping Barrage to cover the advance of their infantry along a portion of the 1st Divisional Front.

3. For this purpose 9 - 18-pdrs. batteries and 2 - 4.5" How, batteries will be placed at the disposal of the C.R.A., 1st Division, as follows :-

    A Group.   A/83, B/83 and A/82
                A/168
                D/83

    B Group.   C/23
                107
                A and B/282
                D/23

    C Group.   A/48.   This battery will be placed under the temporary command of "A" Group for the purpose of this operation to facilitate the passage of orders, and will arrange to link up with the same line of communication as that used by the other batteries of "A" Group via PHEASANT FARM.

4. With the exception of A, and B/83, A/82 and A/48, the above mentioned batteries will revert to their normal tasks and zones at 4 p.m. on the day of attack.
    A and B/83, A/82 and A/48 will remain at the disposal of the C.R.A., 1st Division, for S.O.S. purposes until no longer required by him.

5. An Artillery Liaison Officer detailed by the C.R.A., 1st Division, will be at Headquarters, "B" Group, GOURNIER FARM, throughout the operations for the purpose of passing on the orders of the C.R.A., 1st Division, to the batteries concerned.
    He will be given every facility for using the lines required, and O.C. "A" Group, will send an orderly to H.Q., "B" Group, to collect written orders for his batteries, when required by the Liaison Officer.
    Orders emanating from the C.R.A., 1st Division, for the batteries temporarily on loan will be sent direct to GOURNIER FARM for distribution as above, under arrangements to be made by 1st Divisional Artillery, with whom the Liaison Officer will be in telephonic communication via the 58th Divisional Artillery H.Q. Exchange in the CANAL BANK.

6. All orders for Barrages, S.O.S. Lines, etc. will be communicated direct to the batteries on loan by the above method.
    Registration will be commenced forthwith on points in the area V.23. and V.29.

7. From ZERO till 6 p.m., 2-18 pounder batteries have been detailed by the 17th Divisional Artillery Group to cover the front of the 58th Division from the existing left flank boundary at V.14.a.95.00 - V.14.d.35.60.

8. From /-

8. From ZERO onwards the front covered by the 58th Divisional Artillery Group will be subdivided between Groups as shewn on attached tracing.

At 5 p.m., all units will again fire on the same zones as they did before the operation, with the exception of those mentioned in para. 4, and A and B Groups will distribute their fire so as to cover their whole Group fronts until the remaining batteries are released by 1st Divisional Artillery.

9. The following amount of ammunition must be collected at all battery positions by midday on November 9th, exclusive of the anticipated expenditure for the ensuing 12 hours.

        18-pdrs.   700   (75% shrapnel)
        4.5" Hows.   700   as many 106 fuzes as possible.

The estimated expenditure after ZERO on the day of the attack is 400 and 300 rounds per gun and Howitzer respectively.

10. The remaining units of the 58th Divisional Artillery Group who are not firing a barrage for the 1st Divisional Artillery will put down a barrage along the whole Divisional front, for which orders will be issued separately.

11. ACKNOWLEDGE.

H. Williamson
Captain,
Brigade Major, R.A.,
58th Divisional Arty. Group.

7th November 1917.

Copies to	Copy No.
A Group	1 - 9
B Group	10 - 18
C Group	19 - 27
D Group	28 - 36
R.A. II Corps	37
H.A. II Corps	38
58th Division "G"	39
17th Div. Arty.	40
1st Div. Arty.	41 - 42
32nd Div. Arty.	43
18th Div. Arty.	44
Staff Captain, 18th Div. Arty.	45
Liaison Officer, 175th Inf. Bde.	46
175th Infy. Bde.	47
174th Infy. Bde.	48
173rd Infy. Bde.	49
Staff Captain, R.A.	50
R.O.R.A.	51
Signal Officer R.A.	52
War Diary	53 - 54
File	55 - 56

SECRET.   Copy No......29..

58th Divisional Artillery Group Order No. 63.

1. In continuation of 58th Divisional Artillery Group Order No. 62, a tracing is forwarded herewith giving zones allotted to A and B Groups and the lines upon which the Barrage is to fall.

2. A Time-table of lifts is also attached, Barrage Table "A".

3. A practice Barrage will be carried out on "B" day exactly according to the Tracing and Time-Table, but will cease at 0.27 to save wastage of ammunition.

4. ZERO for the practice Barrage will be 3 p.m., and the most careful registration must be carried out and completed in the course of the morning of "B" day.

5. Further orders will be issued with regard to the Final PROTECTIVE BARRAGE which will be fired in conjunction with the CREEPING BARRAGE shewn on the diagram, when actually covering the Infantry on the day of attack.

6. ACKNOWLEDGE.

H. Williamson
Captain,
Brigade Major, R.A.,
58th Divisional Arty. Group.

8th November 1917.
N.

Distribution :-
A Group	1 - 6
B Group	7 - 13
R.A., II Corps	14
H.A., II Corps	15
58th Division "G"	16
1st Div. Artillery.	17 - 20
17th Div. Artillery	21
32nd Div. Artillery	22
18th Div. Artillery	23
Staff Captain, 18th D.A.	24
Staff Captain, 58th D.A.	25
R.O.R.A.	26
Signal Officer R.A.	27
War Diary	28 - 29
File	30 - 31

Issued with 58th D.A.G.
Order No. 63.

BARRAGE TABLE "A".

1. 0.0   (a) 50% available 18-pdrs in each Group open on the line marked "A" on their own zone and remain till 0.3
       (b) 50% available 18-pdrs in each Group open on the dotted line marked "B"

0.3	(a) and (b)	Lift 100x	and remain till 0.11
0.11	(a) and (b)	Lift 100x	and remain till 0.19
0.19	(a) and (b)	Lift 100x	and remain till 0.27
0.27	(a) and (b)	Lift 100x	and remain till 0.35
0.35	(a) and (b)	Lift 100x	and remain till 0.43
0.43	(a) and (b)	Lift 100x	and remain till 0.51
0.51	(a) and (b)	Lift 100x	

Remaining orders for the final lifts on to the PROTECTIVE BARRAGE will be issued later.

All shrapnel will be used and 50% on graze should be calculated for.

Rate of Fire - 3 rounds per gun per minute.

2. 0.0   All available 4.5" Howitzers open on line "G" and remain till 0.3
   0.3   Lift 100x and continue so doing every 8 minutes always keeping 300x in front of the edge of the CREEPING BARRAGE nearest the Infantry and paying special attention to any strong points shown on Intelligence Maps till 0.51
   0.51   Further orders for the Final P OTECTIVE BARRAGE will be issued later

106 fuzes will be used where available.

Rate of Fire - 2 rounds per How. per minute.

SECRET. Copy No. 49

58th Divisional Artillery Group Order No. 65.

1. The next attack on the enemy's positions will be made on "D" day by 1st (Imperial) Division in conjunction with the Canadian Corps.

2. The 58th Divisional Artillery will co-operate

   (a) By firing an Enfilade CREEPING BARRAGE to cover the advance of the 1st Division's Infantry.
   Orders for this have been issued separately to the 9 - 18-pdr. and 2 - 4.5" How. batteries detailed for the purpose.

   (b) By firing a CREEPING BARRAGE as detailed in Barrage Table "A" with the remaining 18-pdr. and 4.5" How. batteries on part of the 58th Division front.

   (c) by firing a Smoke Screen with 3 - 4.5" How. batteries.

3. A portion of the 58th Division front is being covered by the 57th Divisional Artillery Group and for the purposes of the barrage detailed in para. 2 (b) the front will be divided as on attached tracing.
   This cancels that issued with 58th D.A. Group Order No. 62, but at 4 p.m. on the afternoon of "D" day, with the exception of A and B/83, A/82, and A/48, all Groups revert to their normal zones and tasks as detailed in that order.

4. The Smoke Screen will be fired from 0.0 - 1.10 as follows :-

   V.28.a.7.4. - V.22.d.0.2   by   D/83
   V.22.d.0.2 - V.22.b.0.0   by   D/168
   Superimposed and sweeping up and down from V.28.2.7.4. - V.22.b.0.0   by D/83

5. Rates of fire.

	Rounds per gun per minute.	
	18-pdr.	4.5" How.
0.0 - 0.3	4	2
0.3 - 1.7	2	$1\frac{1}{2}$
1.7 - END	1	$\frac{1}{2}$
Bursts of Fire	2	1

   Smoke Barrage.   Groups of 8, at 200^x interval every 2 minutes.

   18-pounders will use all shrapnel and calculate a corrector to give 50% on graze.

6. A burst of fire will take place from 4.5 - 4.10 p.m. on Selected hostile Tracks and approaches as shewn on Intelligence maps.
   Silent periods will be observed :-
   6.0 p.m. - 6.30 p.m.
   8.0 p.m. - 8.20 p.m.

7. ACKNOWLEDGE.

H. Williams
Captain,
Brigade Major, R.A.,
58th Divisional Arty. Group.

9.11.1917.

SECRET.   Copy No. ....

58th Divisional Artillery Group Order No. 56.

1. The attack on the enemy's positions will be made on "B" Day by 1st (Imperial) Division in conjunction with the Canadian Corps.

2. The 58th Divisional Artillery will co-operate -

   (a) By firing on BARRAGE or CREEPING BARRAGE to cover the advance of the 1st Division Infantry.
       Traces for this barrage are issued separately to the O. 16-pdr., and 2 - 4.5" how. batteries detailed for the purpose.

   (b) By firing a CREEPING BARRAGE as shown on attached Trace "A" with the remainder of the 16-pdr. and 4.5" how. batteries on a front of the 58th Division front.

   (c) By firing a smoke barrage with 2 - 4.5" how. batteries.

3. A portion of the 58th D.A. will be placed at the disposal of the 58th Divisional Artillery Group and "B" Group for the barrages detailed in para. 2 (a) & (b), the 58th D.A. being known as on attached Tracing.

   The amount that is under 58th D.A. Group Order No. 52, but at 4 p.m. on the afternoon of "D" day, with the exception of A and B Gp, A/83, and A/93, all Groups revert to their normal zones and tasks as detailed in that order.

4. The smoke screen will be fired from 6.0 - 1.10 as follows :-

   V.29.b.7.4. - V.23.d.0.0.   by D/83
   V.23.d.0.3. -- V.23.b.0.8. by D/83
   Superimposed and creeping up and down from V.29.B.7.4. -
                  V.23.b.0.0. by D/83

5. Rates of fire.   Rounds per gun per minute.
                                            18-pdr.   4.5" How.

   6.0 - 6.8   3   2
   6.8 - 1.7   2   1½
   1.7 - End   1   1

   Bursts of Fire   2   1

   Smoke Barrage.   Groups of 5, at 200X interval every 2 minutes.

   18-pounders will use all shrapnel and will also a corrector to ½ to 50 on gauge.

6. A burst of fire will take place from 4.5 - 4.10 p.m. on selected hostile Trench and approaches as shown on Intelligence Map.

   Whose periods will be observed :-

      7.0 p.m.   -   6.30 p.m.
      8.6 p.m.   -   8.10 p.m.

7. ACKNOWLEDGE.

                                        (signed) H.W. Williamson
                                        Brigade Major, R.A.
O.1 p.m.   58th Divisional Artly. Group.

Issued with 50 D.A.Group
Order No.65, 9-11-17.

BARRAGE TABLE "A"

0.0.   All available 18 pounders and 4.5" Howitzers will
       come down on a line 250^x from our front line in the zones
       allotted on attached tracing   and remain till 0. 3.

0.3.   Lift 100^x and remain till 0.11.

0.11. Lift 100^x and continue lifting 100^x every
       8 minutes   till 0.59.

0.59. Search back in bursts of fire for 400^x until
       consolidation is completed.

ADDENDUM No.1. to 58th D.A.GROUP ORDER NO.65.

From zero onwards special precaution will be taken by the batteries of "A" and "B" Groups who are supporting the 1st Division, to have a pointer erected in their position which indicates the direction from which a S.O.S. rocket on the 1st Divisional front will come up.

The rocket post of the 1st Divisional Artillery will be at D.7.a.7.5. on the ARBRE ridge.

The pointer must also indicate the front of the 1st Division covered by these batteries, which, if the operations are successful, should be V.23.d.8.2.

ACKNOWLEDGE.

H. Williamson
Captain,
Brigade Major, R.A.
58th Divisional Artillery Group.

9-11-17.

SECRET.   Copy No. 53

58th Divisional Artillery Group Order No. 66.

1. An ARMY Barrage will be fired on "E" day as follows :-

   (a) 0.0   2/3 available 18-pounders open on their
              S.O.S. Lines   and remain till 0.6
       0.6   Lift 100^X and remain till 0.9
       0.9   Lift 100^X and continue so doing every
              3 minutes   till 0.27
       0.27 Drop back on to S.O.S. Lines till   0.30
       0.30 STOP.

   (b) 0.0   1/3 available 18-pounders and all 4.5"
              Hows. open on a line 100^X beyond the
              18-pounder S.O.S. Line and conform with
              (a)   till 0.27
       0.27 (i) 1/3 available 18-pounders) and
              drop 600^X) remain till 0.30
           (ii) All 4.5" Hows. drop 400^X)
       0.30 STOP

2. Rates of fire - NORMAL.

3. Nature of ammunition.   50% H.E. and Shrapnel.

   Corrector calculated to give 50% on graze.

   4.5" Hows. will use 106 Fuze where available.

4. Group Zones as for days previous to "D" day.

5. ZERO Hour at 5.0 a.m.

6. ACKNOWLEDGE.

                              H. Williamson
                              Captain,
                         Brigade Major, R.A.,
9th November 1917.   58th Divisional Artillery Group.

A Group	1 - 9
B Group	10 - 18
C Group	19 - 27
D Group	28 - 36
R.A., II Corps	37
H.A., II Corps	38
58th Division "G"	39
174th Infy. Bde.	40
Liaison Offr. 174th Infy. Bde.	
1st Div. Artillery	42
32nd Div. Arty.	43
57th Div. Arty.	44
18th Div. Arty.	45
Staff Captain, 18 D.A.	46
Staff Captain, 58 D.A.	47
R.O.R.A.	48
Signal Officer R.A.	49
War Diary	50 - 51
File	52 - 53

SECRET   Copy No. ..53..

58th Divisional Artillery Group Order No. 68.

1. Reference 58th Divisional Artillery Group Order No. 37, Appendix 1. Tables for Barrages H (a), 1/4, I (a), and 1/5 are forwarded herewith.

2. Attention is drawn to the fact that, for the present, the Infantry will be endeavouring to patrol up to the line V.14.b.2.1 - V.15.c.3.9. - V.15.c.8.0. - V.21.b.5.2. - V.21.d.4.5. and the Barrages H (a) and I (a) will commence 150^x beyond this line. Barrages 1/4 and 1/5 however will commence as usual on the S.O.S. Line.

3. Should any 18-pounders or 4.5" Howitzers not be able to reach the range necessary to comply with the lifts, they should come back to a line 300^x beyond that from which they started and then start forward again until such time as they can comply with the lifts ordered.

4. ACKNOWLEDGE.

H. Williamson
Captain,
Brigade Major R.A.,
58th Divisional Arty. Group.

12.11.1917.

Distribution as in 58th D.A. Group Order No. 67.

Issued with 58th D.A.
Group Order No. 68.

BARRAGE TABLE.

ARMY BARRAGE "H" (a)
6 a.m. "H" Day.

(a)
0.0	2/3 available 18-pounders open on a line 150ˣ beyond the Infantry patrol line and remain till 0.6
0.6	Lift 200ˣ and remain till 0.9
0.9	Lift 100ˣ and continue doing so every 3 minutes till 0.30
0.30	Drop 600ˣ and remain till 0.33
0.33	STOP.

(b)
0.0	1/3 available 18-pounders and all available 4.5" Howitzers open on a line 100ˣ beyond (a) and remain till 0.9
0.9	Lift 100ˣ and remain till 0.12
0.12	Lift 100ˣ and continue so doing every 3 minutes till 0.30
0.30	Drop 300ˣ and remain till 0.33
0.33	STOP

CORPS BARRAGE 1/5   Issued with 58th D.A.
6.15 a.m. "I" Day.   Group Order No. 68.

BARRAGE TABLE.

(a)   0.0   2/3 available 18-pounders open on line 150^x beyond the
             Infantry patrol line
      0.8   Lift 500^x and remain till   0.8
      0.12   Drop 100^x and remain till   0.12
      0.16   Drop 100^x and remain till   0.16
      0.20   Drop 100^x and remain till   0.20
      0.28   Lift 100^x and remain till   0.28
      0.36   STOP.   and remain till   0.36

(b)   0.0   1/3 available 18-pounders open on a line 100^x beyond (a)
      0.4   Lift 100^x and remain till   0.4
      0.8   Lift 100^x and remain till   0.8
      0.12   Lift 200^x and remain till   0.12
      0.24   Drop 100^x and remain till   0.24
      0.36   STOP.   and remain till   0.36

(c)   0.0   All available 4.5" Howitzers open on a line 100^x beyond (u)
      0.4   Lift 100^x and remain till   0.4
      0.8   Lift 100^x and remain till   0.8
      0.12   Lift 100^x and remain till   0.12
      0.24   Drop 100^x and remain till   0.24
      0.28   Lift 100^x and remain till   0.28
      0.36   STOP.   and remain till   0.36

AMENDMENT to 58th Divisional Arty. Group Order No. 67, Appendix I and 58th D.A. Group Order No. 68.

CORPS BARRAGE 1/4 at 3 p.m. on "H" Day is cancelled.
ARMY BARRAGE I (a) at 6.15 a.m. on "I" Day is cancelled.
CORPS BARRAGE 1/5 on "I" Day will take place at 6.15 a.m. and not at 2.30 p.m.

ACKNOWLEDGE.

                                                        Captain,
                                           Brigade Major, R.A.,
12.11.1917.   58th Divisional Arty. Group.

Copies to all recipients of 58th D.A.G. Order No. 57 and 68.

SECRET.   Copy No. 42

58th Divisional Artillery Group Order No. 69.

Reference Map.   SPRIET Sheet   1/10,000.

---

1. A bombardment of the enemy's front system of defence S. of the SPRIET Road will take place on "I" and "J" Days.

2. The II Corps H.A. are co-operating as follows :-

    0.0 - 1.0   Bombard CAMERON HOUSE
                          MORAY HOUSE

    (0.40 - 0.45   Intense rate of fire.)

    1.0 - 2.0   Concentration on
                     (a) Trench V.21.a.70.95 - V.21.a.85.72
                     (b) PAPA FARM.

    These bombardments are with a view to driving the enemy from their concrete dugouts into the shell-holes which they are known to occupy when any particular dug-out is submitted to an organised bombardment.

3. The action of the 58th Divisional Artillery Group will be as follows :-

    A Group.

    18-pounders.

    0.0 - 1.0   V.21.c.62.68 - V.21.c.85.30   600 Shrapnel.

    0.0 - 1.0   Hedge in front of MORAY HOUSE   180 H.E.

    1.0 - 2.0   Paths and approaches E. of MORAY HOUSE and bursts of fire in the form of a box barrage 200^x N. E. and S. of it.
                                                   800 Shrapnel.

    4.5" Howitzers.

    0.30 - 0.35) Concentrate intense fire on   100 Rounds
    0.40 - 0.45) MORAY HOUSE.   106 fuze.

    1.0 - 1.10) Intense with   ) Old gun emplacements
                     Lethal   )
    1.10 - 1.50) Lachrymatory   ) V.21.d.2.8.

    B Group.

    18-pounders.

    0.0 - 1.0   V.20.b.75.65 - V.20.b.92.31   600 Shrapnel.

    1.0 - 2.0   Paths and approaches E. of PAPA FARM and bursts of fire in the form of a box barrage 200^x N. E. and S. of it   800 Shrapnel.

    4.5" Howitzers. /

2.

4.5" Howitzers.

0.30 - 0.35)	Concentrate intense fire	100 rounds
0.40 - 0.45)	on CAMERON HOUSE.	106 fuzes.
1.0 - 1.10)	Intense with) Lethal	Old gun emplacement
1.10 - 1.50)	Lachrymatory)	V.21.b.2.0

4. Each Group (A and B) will detail one 18-pounder battery to arrange direct communication with the best available O.P. for direct observation on the localities mentioned in para. 3.   WINCHESTER FARM is the most suitable.
The Observing Officer for this Battery will make a special look out for sniping small parties of the enemy dislodged by the bombardment and should make a registration before it begins.

5. ZERO Hour will be 2 p.m.

Should the wind be unfavourable for Gas, this will be notified by wire to all concerned.

6. ACKNOWLEDGE.

H. Williamson
Captain,
Brigade Major, R.A.,
58th Divisional Artillery Group.

14.11.1917.

Distribution as in 58th D.A. Order No. 67.
Copy to Corps Chem. Adviser.

SECRET.   Copy No. 50

58th Divisional Artillery Group Order No. 72.

1. The 58th Division is being relieved in the line by the 35th Division.   Command passes at 10 a.m. on November 17th.

2. The front held by the 58th Division is being extended S.E. to V.28.a.4.2. on the night 17th/18th November.

3. Responsibility for defence of the new front passes to 58th Divisional Artillery Group at 5 p.m. on the 16th.   Zones allotted to Groups are shewn on attached tracing.

4. The front held by the 35th Division will continue to be covered by the 58th Divisional Artillery Group, with the exception of the batteries at present on loan to the 1st. Divisional Artillery Group, who will continue to function for the 1st D.A. Group until further orders.

5. ACKNOWLEDGE.

                                                    H. Williamson
                                                    Captain,
                                                    Brigade Major, R.A.,
16th November 1917.   58th Divisional Arty. Group.

     Distribution :-
            A Group   1 -   9
            B Group   10 - 18
            C Group   19 - 27
            D Group   28 - 36
            R.A., II Corps   37
            H.A., II Corps   38
            58th Division "G"   39
            174th Infy. Bde.   40
            L.O., 174th Infy. Bde.   41
            1st Div. Arty.   42
            32nd Div. Arty.   43
            50th Div. Arty.   44
            18th Div. Arty.   45
            35th Division "G"   46
            Staff Captain, 58th D.A.   47
            R.O.R.A.   48
            Signals Officer R.A.   49
            War Diary   50 - 51
            File   52 - 53

SECRET.   Copy No. ....

58th Divisional Artillery Group Order No. 73.

1. The following Mutual Support will be arranged :-

    (a) In case of attack on front of 17th Division on our left, who are covered by 50th Divisional Artillery Group,

     CODE CALL.   SUPPORT HYTHE.

    Acting by 58th D.A. Group.

    Left Brigade, "D" Group, open on their S.O.S. Lines.
    4 - 4.5" Howitzers of D Group open on SPIDER CROSS ROADS.
    6 - 18 pounder guns of D Group open on road running N.E. through V.9.c.

    (b) In case of attack on front held by 35th Division, who are covered by the 58th D.A. Group,

     CODE CALL.   SUPPORT LONDON.

    Action by 50th D.A. Group.

    Right Brigade of their Right hand Group opens on their S.O.S. Lines
    4 - 4.5" Howitzers open on SPIDER CROSS ROADS.
    12 - 18-pdrs. open on road running N.E. through V.9.c.

2. (a) In case of attack on front held by 1st Imperial Divn.

     CODE CALL.   SUPPORT IMPERIAL.

    Action by 58th D.A. Group.

    Right Brigade of "A" Group (not less than 12 guns) open on S.O.S. Lines on its own Front.

    (b) In case of attack on front held by 35th Division,

     CODE CALL.   SUPPORT LONDON.

    Left flank brigade of Left flank Group, 1st D.A. Group, open on their S.O.S. Lines.

3. In all cases of S.O.S. Signal being sent up, fire will be opened for 10 minutes at 3 rounds per gun per minute, followed by 5 minutes at 2 rounds per gun per minute and then stop, unless the Signal is repeated or a continuance is ordered by Liaison Officer at request of B.G.C. Infantry Brigade, or from D.A.H.Q.   In this case the process will be repeated.
    4.5" Howitzers fire at half above rates.

4. ACKNOWLEDGE.

              H. Williamson
              Captain,
             Brigade Major, R.A.,
16th Novr. 1917.   58th Divisional Arty. Group.

  Distribution as for 58th D.A.G. Order No. 72.

SECRET. Copy No. 22

58th Divisional Artillery Group Order No. 74.

1. The personnel of the 32nd Divisional Artillery will relieve the personnel of 2nd Divisional Artillery under the 1st (Imperial) D.A. Group on November 17th. as follows :-

   (a) H.Q., 2 - 18-pdr. and 1 - 4.5" How. Battery, 168th Brigade R.F.A. will relieve their equivalent of the 41st Bde. R.F.A. in action, and the O.C., 168th Bde. R.F.A., will assume command of No. 2 Group, 1st D.A. Group.

   (b) 3 - 18-pdr. batteries, 161st Bde. R.F.A. relieve their equivalent of the 36th Bde. R.F.A. in action.

   Location statement of 41st and 36th Bdes. R.F.A. is attached.

   Units of 2nd D.A. not in the line will not be relieved. Units of 32nd D.A. who are not relieving will concentrate in their Wagon Lines of which there will be no change of position.

2. Units of 32nd Divisional Artillery will take all gun stores with them as they will be required in the positions handed over to them by the 2nd D.A., but they will hand over their guns and sights complete to the 58th D.A. Group as follows :-

   (a) Units of 161st Bde. R.F.A. will hand over guns and sights complete, history sheets and documents with regard to position to O.C., 126th Army Bde. R.F.A., who will provide a guard to be placed on all positions vacated by them, with the exception of D/161 who will provide their own.

   (b) Units of 168th Bde. R.F.A. will hand over guns and sights complete, history sheets, and documents with regard to position to O.C. "A" Group, who will provide a guard to be placed on all positions vacated by them.

3. Command of "D" Group passes to O.C. 126th Army Bde. R.F.A. at 1 p.m., November 17th.

4. Brigade and Battery Commanders of 32nd D.A. who are going into the line will meet O.C., No. 2 Group, 1st (Imperial) D.A. Group, at 10 a.m. at HACKNEY VILLA, C.12.c.0.2., to make all necessary arrangements for carrying out the relief.

5. Orders for re-distribution of 58th D.A. Group front, re-manning positions and withdrawal of guns will be issued later.

6. Completion of taking over the positions vacated by units of 32nd D.A. will be wired to this Office by "A" Group and "D" Group.
   The number of guns fit, and unfit, for action being stated in each case.

7. ACKNOWLEDGE.

H. Williamson
Captain,
Brigade Major, R.A.,
58th Divisional Arty. Group.

17th November 1917.

Distribution.

DISTRIBUTION :-

A Group	1
B Group	2
C Group	3
D Group	4
120th Army Bde. R.F.A.	5
168th Bde. R.F.A.	6
R.A., II Corps	7
H.A., II Corps	8
35th Division "G"	9
106th Infy. Bde.	10
L.O., 106th Infy. Bde.	11
1st Div. Arty.	12
No. 2 Group, 1st D.A.	13
32nd Div. Arty.	14
50th Div. Arty.	15
18th Div. Arty.	16
S.C., 58th D.A. Group	17
S.C., 58th Div. Arty.	18
R.O.R.A.	19
Signal Officer R.A.	20
War Diary	21 - 22
File	23 - 24

LOCATION STATEMENT OF

No. 2 GROUP, 1st (IMPERIAL) D.A. GROUP.

	Position.	Wagon Lines.
No. 2 Group Headquarters. 41st Bde. R.F.A. (2nd Divn.) Lt. Col. J.G. DOONER.	C.12.c.0.2 (HACKNEY VILLA)	C.25.c.
9th Battery R.F.A.	C.12.b.6.4.)	
16th Battery R.F.A.	Wagon Lines)	
17th Battery R.F.A.	C.12.b.5.6.)	C.25.c.
47th (How.) Btty. R.F.A.	C.12.d.8.5.)	
36th Bde. R.F.A. (2nd Divn. H.Qrs. Lt. Col. A.A. GOSHEN, D.S.O.		B.27.c.0.4.
15th Battery R.F.A.	C.12.c.1.4.	H.5.c.7.6.
48th Battery R.F.A.	D.7.a.1.3.	H.5.b.8.5.
71st Battery R.F.A.	C.12.d.3.3.	H.5.b.5.2.
D/36th Btty. R.F.A.	Wagon Lines	B.30.d.2.8.

HQ RO 58
DECEMBER 1917

Army Form C 2118.

WAR DIARY
or
INTELLIGENCE SUMMARY.
(Erase heading not required.)

Instructions regarding War Diaries and Intelligence Summaries are contained in F.S. Regs., Part II. and the Staff Manual respectively. Title pages will be prepared in manuscript.

Place	Date	Hour	Summary of Events and Information	Remarks and references to Appendices
ETAPLES AREA	4th		The Divisional Artillery moved by road to II Corps Area, staying on this day in THIEMBRONE AREA	
	5th		Moved by road to LEDERZEELE - ST MOMELIN AREA.	
	6th		G.O.C.R.A. 58th Division assumed command of the Artillery covering the 35th Divisional front, taking over from G.O.C., R.A. 63rd Division on right sector and G.O.C., R.A. 50th Division on the left. Headquarters were situated at CANAL BANK. Brigades and D.A.C. marched to ZERMEZEELE AREA.	
	7th		Brigades and D.A.C. marched to wagon lines in ELVERDINGHE AREA.	
	9th & 10th		Brigades went into the line covering 58th Division as follows:- 290th Brigade R.F.A. relieved 82nd and 83rd Brigades R.F.A. (18th Divisional Artillery) with Headquarters at CANE POST. 291st Brigade R.F.A. 250th and 251st Brigades (50th Divisional Artillery) with Headquarters at ADELPHI HOUSE. 34th and 48th Army Brigades R.F.A. were also in the 58th D.A.G.	
	14th/15th		48th Army Brigade R.F.A. left 58th Divisional Artillery group.	
			During this period harrassing fire has been continuously carried out. Much progress has been made in salving guns and ammunition.	

Smith
Brigadier General, R.A.
Commanding, 58th Divisional Artillery.

WAR DIARY or INTELLIGENCE SUMMARY

Army Form C. 2118.

For month of January 1918.

58th D^{nl} Artillery

Sheet 1

Place	Date	Hour	Summary of Events and Information	Remarks and references to Appendices
AMIEL BANK outs^k of BOUES MESNIL	1st to 8th		"Defensive" operation only carried out	
	9		H.Q. 58th D.A. were relieved in the line by 35th D.A. & H.Q. 58th D.A. on the same day at Tenthurs camp close to POPERINGHE	
	10/13 12/14		Batteries of 58th D.A. were relieved in the line by batteries of the 35th D.A.	
	22		Instr^{ns} recd at PROVEN H.Q. established at CORBIE on transfer from II Corps 4th Army to III Corps 5th Army	
	23		H.Q. closed at CORBIE & opened at ERCHEU	
	26		H.Q. " " " ERCHEU " " CHAUNY	
	28		190 & 291 Brigades RFA (and 5th D.A. R.H.A. attached) marched to Roye area from CORBIE	3 RD.A.C
	29		The same units marched to VARENNES, BEBOEUF, HANGARD, DOMART area, MONTECOURT area	
	30		58th D.A. and 5th Bde. R.H.A. Relieved 62nd French Artillery & 5th French Cavalry Division	
	31		Regⁿ of guns by Battery Commanders commenced. Brought II CRA 58th D.A. at 6 p.m.	

Maxwell
CRA 58th D.A.

WAR DIARY or INTELLIGENCE SUMMARY.

58th D.U. Artillery Army Form C. 2118.

for February 1918

Place	Date	Hour	Summary of Events and Information	Remarks and references to Appendices
HQ ROUEZ	1		The 58th Div. Art. took over from the French on the 1st inst. and at once proceeded	
VENDEUIL	5		to organise the defence Reserve positions for defending the Battle Zone were commenced also Reinforcing positions. No operations were undertaken during the period a purely defensive attitude was	
LA FERE	28		adopted very little firing be carried out	
BARISIS			The enemy's attitude has been quiet for the month VENDEUIL TERGNIER & BARISIS receiving some attention from time to time. On days of good visibility there was considerable activity by enemy aircraft.	
			On 27th inst the 5 RHA left the D. unaccompanied the unusual 918 D.A. which however there has not been our return a C. Brigade Group French	

Maxwell
Brig General
CRA. 58 D.A.

WAR DIARY or INTELLIGENCE SUMMARY.

(Erase heading not required.)

Army Form C. 2118.

Place	Date	Hour	Summary of Events and Information	Remarks and references to Appendices
	Feb. 3		Captain W.H. Lazenby (Adjutant) proceeded on a month's leave. 5th Army Brigade R.H.A. took over Centre Sector (consisting of "A" and "Z" Batteries R.H.A.) from 6 p.m.	
	Feb. 6		2 guns of D/290 came into action after dark in the position selected for the Battery in the BOIS VIVIER.	
	Feb. 8		G.O.C. R.A. III Corps inspected the sites selected for "Battle Zone" positions and O.P.s, and made one or two minor alterations. Relief of 2nd Infantry Brigade (30th Div.) by 175th Brigade (58th Div.) in the VENDEUIL sector was completed today. Extract from 58 Divnl. O.Rn. N° 9/18. " BELGIAN CROIX DE GUERRE — was awarded to N° 925344 Sergt 224 Bondarens A/290, N° 925593 Corpl. H.E. Butler B/290, and N° 925578 Bomber J. Parsons B/290.	
	Feb. 15		2/Lieut A.C. Gill joined from Base, also 2/Lieut H. Marshal, on his appointment, and were posted to A/290 & C/290 respectively. N° 512855 R.S.M. J. Larkin joined from LUTON. B & C/290 took part in a short bombardment of M.O.Y from 3 to 3.30 p.m.	

58 Div Arty

Army Form C. 2118.

WAR DIARY
INTELLIGENCE SUMMARY.

(Erase heading not required.)

Headquarters, 58th Divisional Artillery.

Place	Date	Hour	Summary of Events and Information	Remarks and references to Appendices
	March.			
QUIERZY.	1st - 6th.		German Artillery very quiet. Our offensive action increased and preparation of battle positions and reinforcing positions was accelerated.	
"	Evening 4th.		ST.FIRMIN bombed in conjunction with III Corps H.A.	
	7th - 13th.		Offensive Artillery action on both sides increased. Still further progress made with Battle and Reinforcing positions. ST.FIRMIN Bridges and other vulnerable targets and working parties engaged frequently.	
	Night 10/11th.		D.A. assisted French in local raid on LE CROTOIR.	
	13th - 20th.		Enemy Artillery decreased, being more active on 18th when considerable amount of shelling of back areas took place. Our Artillery continued to keep harassing fire up during the night. Aerial activity was very pronounced on suitable days.	
	19th.		407th and 408th batteries came under tactical control of this D.A.	
	20th.		Fairly quiet night on both sides. A thick mist lay in all low-lying ground.	
	Morning 21st.		At 4.30 a.m. heavy enemy bombardment of front line system and forward areas, gas being used frequently. During the morning enemy advanced towards CROZAT CANAL opposite ST.FIRMIN GATE, but was three times repulsed by Artillery fire. At dusk, under cover of a heavy mist,	

Army Form C. 2118.

WAR DIARY (cont) 2.
or
INTELLIGENCE SUMMARY.
(Erase heading not required.)

Instructions regarding War Diaries and Intelligence Summaries are contained in F. S. Regs., Part II. and the Staff Manual respectively. Title pages will be prepared in manuscript.

Place	Date	Hour	Summary of Events and Information	Remarks and references to Appendices
			the enemy advanced; batteries were withdrawn some distance and came into action again. 2 batteries of 290th Brigade were unable to draw the guns out as the enemy were on top of them. These guns were blown up. All the detachments were withdrawn with the exception of 2 who were captured by the enemy. Enemy holding line along CROZAT CANAL.	
	22nd.		4 Trench Mortars (6" Stokes) captured by enemy. 2 Officers and 2 N.C.Os missing. Enemy crossed canal opposite TERGNIER and by sheer weight of numbers took the town. Batteries firing under forward observation caused the enemy considerable losses, and delayed him. Batteries of 291st Brigade Group on south bank of River OISE inflicted heavy losses on enemy by enfilade fire. At dusk batteries of 290th Brigade retired further West.	
	23rd.		3 a.m. batteries north of River OISE opened a sweeping barrage along the front but enemy again forced the infantry to fall back. At 1 p.m. Northern batteries (290th Brigade) retired to GAUMONT and opened fire on VIRY NOREUIL - NOREUIL front. Southern batteries,(291st Brigade) harassed enemy advance considerably causing much damage to transport and personnel.	
	24th.		R.A.H.Q. closed at QUIERZY and opened at VARENNES, but subsequently moved to CAMELIN.	

T.J134. Wt. W708-776. 500000. 4/15. Sir J. C. & S.

Army Form C. 2118.

WAR DIARY (cont) 3.
or
INTELLIGENCE SUMMARY.
(Erase heading not required.)

Instructions regarding War Diaries and Intelligence Summaries are contained in F. S. Regs., Part II. and the Staff Manual respectively. Title pages will be prepared in manuscript.

Place	Date	Hour	Summary of Events and Information	Remarks and references to Appendices
CAMELIN.	24th.		Northern batteries (290 Brigade) withdrawn to positions near BETHANCOURT-en-VAUX but enemy advanced more quickly and they had to withdraw further to positions near CREPIGNY. At dusk batteries (290 Brigade) withdrawn to BABOEUF. During the day the Artillery fire from all the batteries inflicted very heavy losses on the enemy. Trench Mortars attached to Right Group moved to BICHANCOURT and subsequently moved with 58th D.A.G. whose movements conformed with the movement and requirements of Brigades during the remainder of the month.	
"	25th.		At noon 18th D.A. batteries moved South and crossed to South bank of River OISE. Northern batteries (290 Brigade) took up positions S.E. of VARENNES but these positions becoming untenable they moved to positions in RUEMILLON. Harassing fire was kept up by 291st Brigade batteries during the day and night.	
"	26th.		Northern batteries (290 Brigade) fell back on CUTS in the early morning and then moved to positions in BOIS de MANICAMP. At night, 2 sections of all Southern batteries (291 Brigade) were withdrawn from AMIGNY SECTOR and came into action in area BOIS de FEVE. Harassing fire by both Brigades all night. R.A.H.Q. moved from CAMELIN to BLERAN COURT.	
BLERAN COURT	27th.		Batteries fired on all possible targets. At dusk 291st Brigade Sections returned to AMIGNY	

Army Form C. 2118.

WAR DIARY
or
INTELLIGENCE SUMMARY.

(Erase heading not required.) (cont) 3.

Place	Date	Hour	Summary of Events and Information	Remarks and references to Appendices
BLERAN COURT.	27th.		Sector leaving 2 Howitzers and 1-18 pdr. with 290th Brigade. Harassing fire on enemy lines of communication during the night.	
"	28th.		Batteries organised on 4 gun basis but still in action. Harassing fire at night on roads &c.	
	29th.			
	30th.		Observed fire by day. Harassing fire by night on enemy lines of communication etc.	
	31st.			

Maxwell
Brigadier General, R.A.
C.R.A., 58th Division.

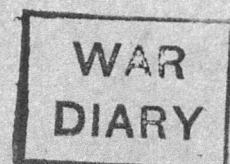

Headquarters,

    58th DIVISIONAL ARTILLERY.

        A P R I L

          1 9 1 8

Army Form C. 2118.

WAR DIARY
INTELLIGENCE SUMMARY.
(Erase heading not required.)

58th Divisional Artillery.

for month of April. 1918.

Instructions regarding War Diaries and Intelligence Summaries are contained in F. S. Regs, Part II. and the Staff Manual respectively. Title pages will be prepared in manuscript.

Place	Date	Hour	Summary of Events and Information	Remarks and references to Appendices
BLERAN COURT.	1st/2nd.		Fairly quiet. Harassing fire was carried out by all batteries on roads, tracks, etc. North of the River Oise between CHAUNY and AMIGNY ROUY. Hostile Artillery quiet. Slight shelling of towns in back areas.	
	2nd/3rd.		290th and 291st Brigades R.F.A. relieved by French Batteries, concentrated in BRIGKK BLERAN COURT prior to march to entraining station.	
	3rd/4th.		290th Brigade followed by 291st Brigade, 58th D.A.C., and 58th T.M. Batteries march to LONGPORT and VILLERS COTTERETS and entrained for LONGEAU. 58th D.A.H.Q. entrained at LONGPORT.	
CAGNY.	4th/5th.		290th, 291st Brigades, 58th D.A.C. and 58th T.M. Batteries detrained at LONGEAU and camped on the BOULEVARDS, AMIENS. 58th D.A.H.Q. detrained at BACOUEL and marched to CAGNY.	
	5 - 7th.		290th and 291st Brigades relieved 16th D.A. in the line covering VILLERS BRETONNEUX and came under orders of 5th Australian D.A. 5th Australian D.A.H.Q. at BLANGY TRONVILLE. 58th D.A.C. less S.A.A. Section moved to GLISY and came under orders of 5th Australian D.A.	
BOVES.	8 - 9th.		58th D.A.H.Q. moved to BOVES in the line under 18th Division. Battery positions of 290th Brigade R.F.A. from 66th Div. Arty, were heavily shelled and some gas on forward areas.	
	10 - 13th.		61st D.A. relieved 39th D.A. on the nights 12/13th and 13/14th. 58th D.A.H.Q. closed at	

T.131. Wt. W708-776. 500000. 4/15. Sir J. C. & S.

Army Form C. 2118.

WAR DIARY
or
INTELLIGENCE SUMMARY.
(Erase heading not required.)

Instructions regarding War Diaries and Intelligence Summaries are contained in F. S. Regs., Part II. and the Staff Manual respectively. Title pages will be prepared in manuscript.

Place	Date	Hour	Summary of Events and Information	Remarks and references to Appendices
			(2) cont.	
FORT MANIOR FARM.			BOVES and re-opened at FORT MANIOR FARM.	
	14 - 18th.		Very little hostile activity. Harassing fire during nights and Counter-preparation fired in the early morning. 4, 6" Newton T.M.s in action close to VILLERS BRETONNEUX. 290th Brigade commenced mutual relief with 298th Army Brigade in the line covering VILLERS BRETONNEUX and came under orders of 58th D.A.	
	19 - 20th.		Relief by 290th Brigade completed and No.1. Section, 58th. D.A.C. came under orders of 58th D.A. The 4, 6" Newton T.M.s withdrawn as positions were full of gas. Concentration shoots were carried out on selected targets behind enemy front line. 2 6" T.M.s put into GENTELLES with 160 rounds of ammunition.	
	21 - 23rd.		Concentration shoots and gas bombardments carried out on selected targets in the enemy's line with good effect. 2 6" T.M.s taken over from 61st D.A. In action in HANGARD fired 62 rounds. 58th D.T.M.O. handed over 2, 6" T.M.s in exchange. O.C., 290th Brigade R.F.A. took over command of the 96th, 169th, and 290th Brigades and established his H.Q. at the H.Q. of 175th Infantry Brigade.	
	24th - 25th.		Enemy attacked our line between VILLERS BRETONNEUX and HANGARD after a heavy bombardment which included much gas. As the Infantry were driven back the forward batteries of 290th and	

T.134. Wt. W708-776. 500000. 4/15. Sir J. C. & S.

Army Form C. 2118.

WAR DIARY
or
INTELLIGENCE SUMMARY.
(Erase heading not required.)

Instructions regarding War Diaries and Intelligence Summaries are contained in F. S. Regs., Part II. and the Staff Manual respectively. Title pages will be prepared in manuscript.

Place	Date	Hour	Summary of Events and Information	Remarks and references to Appendices
			(3) cont.	
			291st Brigades were withdrawn slightly. The same night a successful counter-attack was launched and these batteries moved forward again to their original positions. The artillery fire and barrage inflicted terrible losses on the enemy during the attack. On the 25th 290th Brigade R.F.A. was relieved by the 82nd Brigade R.F.A. and occupied reserve positions just behind. Hostile Artillery was very active during this period.	
	26 - 27th.		All 6" T.M.s were withdrawn from action. Artillery active on both sides. 58th D.A.H.Q. were relieved by 18th D.A.H.Q. and moved to CAGNY.	
	28 - 29th.		291st Brigade was relieved by 86th Army Brigade and proceeded to camp near CAGNY. 290th Brigade withdrew from Reserve positions to the same camp. 58th D.A.H.Q. moved to Fourth Army Rest Area and billeted in FRANCIERES.	
	29 - 30th.		290th and 291st Brigades, 58th D.A.C. and 58th T.M. Batteries march to rest area, staying the night in the CROUY area, and were billeted around EAU COURT.	

Brigadier General, R.A.;
C.R.A., 58th Division.

Army Form C. 2118.

WAR DIARY
INTELLIGENCE SUMMARY

Month of May 1918.

Headquarters, 58th Divisional Artillery.

(Erase heading not required.)

Instructions regarding War Diaries and Intelligence Summaries are contained in F.S. Regs., Part II. and the Staff Manual respectively. Title pages will be prepared in manuscript.

Place	Date	Hour	Summary of Events and Information	Remarks and references to Appendices
FRANCIERES.	1/5/18.		58th Divisional Artillery remained at rest in the 4th Army R.A. rest area. Refitting and a training programme was carried out during this period.	
-do-	6th.		S.A.A. Section, 58th D.A.C. marched from EAUCOURT-sur-SOMME and joined 173rd Infantry Brigade transport column at BOURDON.	
-do-	7th.		S.A.A. Section marched from BOURDON to CONTAY and remained under orders of 58th Division.	
-do-	11th.		B/290th Brigade R.F.A. proceeded by road to SAILLY-le-SEC to act as depot battery at the Reserve Army Artillery School.	
-do-	13th.		Major-General C.B.D. BUDWORTH, C.B.,C.M.G.,M.V.O., B.O.C.R.A. 4th Army inspected the horse lines and gunparks of the 290th and 291st Brigades R.F.A. and 58th D.A.C.	
-do-	15th.		58th D.T.M.O. proceeded to WARLOY to arrange about relief of the 47th Div. T.M. Batteries.	
-do-	16th.		290th Brigade, less "B" Battery, 291st Brigade, and 58th D.A.C., less S.A.A. Section, proceeded by road to BOURDON where they rested for the night. 58th T.M. Batteries proceeded by motor lorry to WARLOY.	
CONTAY.	17th.		H.Q., 58th D.A. proceeded to CONTAY and at 10 a.m. the G.O.C.R.A. took over from the G.O.C.R.A., 47th Division, the command of the artillery covering the 58th Divisional Front. 290th, 291st Brigades and 58th D.A.C. proceeded by road to area around CONTAY	

WAR DIARY
or
INTELLIGENCE SUMMARY.
(Erase heading not required.)

Army Form C. 2118.

Place	Date	Hour	Summary of Events and Information	Remarks and references to Appendices
CONTAY.	17th.		and one section per battery relieved 1 section of the batteries in the line, 290th Brigade relieving the 169th Brigade and 291st Brigade relieving the 282nd Brigade R.F.A. 6, 6" T.M.s and ammunition were taken over from the D.T.M.O., 47th Division in the line.	
-do-	18th.		290th and 291st Brigades R.F.A. completed relief of 169 and 282nd Brigades R.F.A. 407th Battery R.F.A. remained under orders of 290th Brigade R.F.A. to replace B/290. D.T.M.O., 58th Division handed over 6, 6" T.M.s and ammunition to D.T.M.O., 47th Division. "G" Battery R.H.A. attached to 291st Brigade R.F.A. covering the Northern part of the 58th Divisional Sector.	
-do-	19th-30th		Bursts of fire on roads and tracks, counter-preparation and nightfiring programmes carried out. T.M.s carried out shoots on hostile trenches and T.M. emplacements. During the period hostile Artillery was not above normal. Intermittent shelling of front areas was carried out, 4 T.M.s and a small percentage of gas shell used. 4 T.M.s put into rear positions and ammunition dumped near them.	
-do-	25th.		407th Battery R.F.A. relieved by A/236 Brigade.	
-do-	29th.		A/236 Battery was relieved by A/83rd Battery.	
-do-	31st.		291st Brigade R.F.A. assisted 35th Division on left flank during an operation against AVELUY WOOD. Hostile Artillery was more active during the early morning, a large number of	

T.134. Wt. W708-776. 500000. 4/15. Sir J.C. & S.

Army Form C. 2118.

WAR DIARY
or
INTELLIGENCE SUMMARY.
(Erase heading not required.)

Instructions regarding War Diaries and Intelligence Summaries are contained in F. S. Regs., Part II. and the Staff Manual respectively. Title pages will be prepared in manuscript.

Place	Date	Hour	Summary of Events and Information	Remarks and references to Appendices
CONTAY	31st		Phosgene and Green Cross shells being fired into the area around HENEN COURT.	

5th June 1918.

Maxwell
Brigadier General, R.A.
Commanding, 58th Divisional Artillery.

Army Form C. 2118

WAR DIARY
or
INTELLIGENCE SUMMARY.
(Erase heading not required.)

Instructions regarding War Diaries and Intelligence Summaries are contained in F. S. Regs., Part II. and the Staff Manual respectively. Title pages will be prepared in manuscript.

Headquarters, 58th Divisional Artillery.
June 1918.

VR/6

Place	Date	Hour	Summary of Events and Information	Remarks and references to Appendices
CONTAY.	2nd		B.G.R.A. 18th Division took over command of the Field Artillery covering the Left Sector III Corps front at 10 a.m. from B.G.R.A. 58th Division. H.Q.R.A. moved to BAVELINCOURT.	
BAVELINCOURT.	7th.		290 and 291st Brigades R.F.A. relieved in the himself Left Sector, III Corps front on 7th and night 7/8th by 189 and 108 Army Brigades R.F.A. respectively, and withdrew to wagon lines.	
"	8th.		H.Q.R.A. and 290 and 291 Brigades R.F.A. moved to rest area West of AMIENS. The Brigades, D.A.C. and H.Q. marched via MOLLIENS-AU-BOIS, BERTANGLES, to ST. SAVEUR, ARGOEUVES, and D.A.C. to LONGPRE.	
GOEUVES.	10th.		B/290 Battery rejoined their Brigade on return from Fourth Army Artillery School.	
"	11th.		A programme of riding and driving drill and elementary staff work was commenced today by all batteries. Weather hot and fine.	
"	12th.		Weather fine, Brigades - programme as yesterday. Reconnaissance of French front by Bty. Commanders.	
"	13th.		The same.	
"	14th 3.45pm.		G.O.C. 58th Division, Major General Ramsay, C.M.G., D.S.O. visited the 290th Brigade R.F.A. with G.O.C., R.A.	
"	15/16.		Brigades carried out driving and riding drill. Weather hot.	
"	16th.		G.O.C. Division, Major General Ramsay, visited No.2 Section, 58th D.A.C. with G.O.C., R.A.	
"	17th		G.O.C.,R.A. and B.M.,R.A. visited BEAUCOURT CHATEAU and G.O.C.,R.A. went up to see Battery	

Army Form C. 2118.

WAR DIARY
or
INTELLIGENCE SUMMARY.
(Erase heading not required.)

Instructions regarding War Diaries and Intelligence Summaries are contained in F.S. Regs., Part II. and the Staff Manual respectively. Title pages will be prepared in manuscript.

Place	Date	Hour	Summary of Events and Information	Remarks and references to Appendices
ARGOEUVES.	18th.		Positions and Brigade H.Q. that the Divisional Artillery will take over on the relief. Brigade and Battery Commanders visited the Brigades and Batteries they are to relieve in the line on night of 20/21st.	
"	19th		Brigades marched via POULAINVILLE and VILLERS BOCAGE to BEAUCOURT Area.	
"	20th		H.Q.R.A. moved to BEAUCOURT CHATEAU at 10 a.m. and took over command from 47th Div.Arty on rel ief.	
BEAUCOURT.	21st.		Relief of all 47th Divisional Artillery completed.	
"	22/23rd.		G.O.C. Division visited Brigades and Batteries in the line with G.O.C.,R.A. on 23rd and expressed himself as very much pleased with what he saw.	
"	24/25th.		Quiet days with little shelling. Weather fine.	
"	26th.		Hostile Aircraft flew over back areas at 11.15 p.m. A few bombs were dropped.	
"	27/28th.		Quiet days. Some back area shelling by long range guns, and E.A. dropped bombs by night.	
"	29th		The D.A.C. hold sports at BEHEN COURT CHATEAU and had fine weather for a good show.	
"	30th		Flank Division (18th) carried out a successful operation and consolidated their gains. 58th Divisional Artillery co-operated.	

Maxwell
Brigadier General,
C.R.A. 58th Division.

Army Form C. 2118.

WAR DIARY
INTELLIGENCE-SUMMARY
(Erase heading not required.)

Instructions regarding War Diaries and Intelligence Summaries are contained in F.S. Regs., Part II. and the Staff Manual respectively. Title pages will be prepared in manuscript.

Headquarters, 58th Div. Artillery.   July 1918.

Vol 19

Place	Date	Hour	Summary of Events and Information	Remarks and references to Appendices
BEAUCOURT	July 1st.		On night June 30th/July 1st the batteries of this Divisional Artillery assisted in operations carried out by the Divisions on either flank, i.e. 12th and 18th Division on left, and 5th Australian Division on right.	
"	2nd.		Support given to Left flank Division (18th) during hostile attack.	
"	4th.		Barrage fired by units of Divisional Artillery in conjunction with successful attack and capture of enemy trenches on our right by the Australian Corps.	
"	5th.		Units of Divisional Artillery co-operated in Gas Projector operation against enemy trenches. Brigadier General Johnson, C.B., C.M.G., D.S.O., visited C/291 in MERICOURT L'ABBE and expressed great satisfaction at everything he saw.	
"	8th.		Practice manning of Battle Stations carried out. Results were good.	
"	9th.		Gas Bombardment of enemy trenches carried out in co-operation with H.A.	
"	10th.		A & C/108 Bde. R.F.A. attached to 291st Brigade R.F.A. (Right Group)	
"	"		B/108 relieved 377th Battery R.F.A.	
"	14th.		A & D/108 withdrawn to Wagon Lines.	
"	21st.		Gas bombardment of enemy trenches carried out.	
"	25th.		Protective Barrage fired for daylight raid by 2/8th London Regiment (17 prisoners taken by	

Army Form C. 2118.

WAR DIARY
or
INTELLIGENCE SUMMARY.
(Erase heading not required.)

Instructions regarding War Diaries and Intelligence Summaries are contained in F.S. Regs., Part II. and the Staff Manual respectively. Title pages will be prepared in manuscript.

- 2 -

Place	Date	Hour	Summary of Events and Information	Remarks and references to Appendices
BEAUCOURT.	25th.		raiding party.)	
"	26/27th.		Divisional front side-slipped further South.	
"	27/28th.		108th Army Brigade R.F.A. transferred to 47th D.A.	
"	28th.		5th Army Brigade R.H.A. and 86th Army Brigade R.H.A. attached to this Divisional Artillery. Two Chinese attacks made in support of raid by 5th Australian Division.	
"	29th.		A & C/86th Army Brigade R.F.A. joined Right Group.	
"	31st.		All batteries of 86th Army Brigade R.F.A. withdrawn into Wagon Lines into Mobile Reserve. During the whole period the Field Artillery carried out harassing fire on enemy tracks and communications, neutralising enemy T.Ms and counter-battery work. The 6" Trench Mortars were very active throughout the month, taking part in all operations and successfully neutralising enemy T.Ms on several occasions.	

[signature]
Brigadier General,
C.R.A., 58th Division.

58th Divl. Artillery

C. R. A.

58th DIVISION,

AUGUST, 1918.

Army Form C. 2118.

WAR DIARY

Reference Sheets 62.D. and 62.C.

Instructions regarding War Diaries and Intelligence Summaries are contained in F.S. Regs., Part II. and the Staff Manual respectively. Title pages will be prepared in manuscript.

INTELLIGENCE—SUMMARY. August 1918.

(Erase heading not required.)

Headquarters, 58th Div. Arty.

Place	Date	Hour	Summary of Events and Information	Remarks and references to Appendices
BEAUCOURT.	1/2nd.		58th Divisional Artillery relieved in the line, Right Sector, III Corps by 25th D.A. and concentrated in Wagon Lines in neighbourhood of BAVELINCOURT.	
	2nd.		During a reconnaissance, 1 Brigade Cdr. 3, Battery Cdrs, and 1 Battery Captain were wounded, 1 Battery Commander subsequently dying and 1 Battery Commander was killed.	
	3rd.		Batteries commenced dumping ammunition at selected Battery Positions in readiness for offensive operations, at 600 rounds per gun.	
	4th.		At 10 a.m. command of Field Artillery covering Right Sector, III Corps passed to C.R.A., 25th Division. H.Q.R.A. moved from BEAUCOURT to QUERRIEU CHATEAU.	
QUERRIEU.	6th.		Enemy raid penetrated positions selected and new ones had therefore to be chosen for certain batteries at very short notice, 600 rounds per gun having to be got up during the night immediately preceding the attack. This was done.	
	7th.		All batteries moved into action after dusk, all Headquarters taking up battle positions. The Artillery at the disposal of G.O.C., 58th Division, for the attack consisted of 50th D.A., 58th D.A., and 86th Army Brigade R.F.A.	
J.9.c.9.5.	8th.		Attack commenced. For details see Appendix "A".	Appendix "A"

WAR DIARY
or
INTELLIGENCE SUMMARY.
(Erase heading not required.)

Army Form C. 2118.

Place	Date	Hour	Summary of Events and Information	Remarks and references to Appendices
J.26.	12th.		H.Q.R.A. moved to J.26. on appointment of C.R.A., 58th Division as C.R.A., Liaison Force, which was a composite buffer force to link up flanks of III Corps and Aust. Corps. The Artillery covering this composite force was 58th D.A. with 5th Army Brigade R.H.A. attached. The force carried out minor patrol work in the ETINEHEM PENINSULA with the object of capturing BRAY. Important traffic centre in BRAY was gassed by "Z" Special Coy, R.E. on the morning of 17th, the Artillery assisting by a special bombardment.	
	20th.		Liaison Force ceased to exist, being relieved by 3rd Australian Division, which took over the Brigades of this D.A. H.Q.R.A. advanced, closed down and returned to Rear H.Q. at QUERRIEU CHATEAU.	
	22nd. } 24th.		Barrages were fired in support of Infantry attacks, culminating in the capture of BRAY-SUR-SOMME by Australian Infantry on 24/8/18.	
	25th.		H.Q.R.A. advanced opened at K.14.b., South of MORLANCOURT, Rear H.Q., remaining at QUERRIEU CHATEAU.	
	31st.		The D.A. Group covered the attacks of the 58th Division advancing positions from time to time as required. Vide Appendix "B"	App. "B"
	28th.		H.Q.R.A. advanced moved to L.1.b. and H.Q.R.A. Rear, moved to K.14.b.	

Army Form C. 2118.

WAR DIARY
or
INTELLIGENCE SUMMARY.

(Erase heading not required.)

Instructions regarding War Diaries and Intelligence Summaries are contained in F. S. Regs., Part II. and the Staff Manual respectively. Title pages will be prepared in manuscript.

Place	Date	Hour	Summary of Events and Information	Remarks and references to Appendices
	30th.		3.	
			H.Q.R.A. Advanced moved to A.19.b.5.2. and H.Q.R.A. Rear moved to L.l.b.	
			F. Maxwell	
			Brigadier General,	
			C.R.A., 58th Division.	

PRECIS OF OPERATIONS
from 8th to 12th August 1918.

Reference Sheet 62.D.N.E. 1/20,000.

GENERAL PLAN.

The 50th and 58th Divisional Artilleries (under the command of C.R.A., 58th Division) and 86th Army Brigade R.F.A. covered the attack of the 58th Division on the front K.25.a.92.70 - J.36.c.0.0., with their first objective K.27.b.90.50 - K.27.d.90.00 - K.33.c.87.30 and final objective (approx.) Road running through K.22.a.00.75 - K.33.c.0.0 - K.29.a.5.5.

EXECUTION.

8.8.18.   Positions had been carefully reconnoitred in the Forward Area for this attack, but, owing to a German raid in the area selected on 6th August (in which 2 of our gunners were captured, of whom one afterwards escaped), these positions could not be occupied.

New positions were therefore selected at the last minute, batteries were moved up during the night and in position by midnight, 7th/8th August, as follows :-

```
290th Bde. R.F.A.      J.22.d.   and  J.28.c.
291st Bde. R.F.A.      J.28.b.
250th Bde. R.F.A.      J.16.d.
251st Bde. R.F.A.      J.22.b.
 86th Army Bde. R.F.A. J.23.c.
```

Forward Wagon Lines were established E. of the River ANCRE between BONNAY and HEILLY, for the replenishment of ammunition.

The Barrage opened at 4.20 a.m. on the 8th. The Infantry report that the barrage was good, and from the reports of F.O.O.s it appeared well-timed and even. Visibility was impossible during the early part of the morning owing to a thick mist, which was favourable to our Infantry, prisoners stating that the attack was a complete surprise. There was hardly any reply to our barrage by the enemy Field Artillery and hostile Counter-battery work on our positions was nil. A smoke barrage was employed from /

from Zero to Zero plus 4 hours on the line K.9.a.8.6 - K.10.a.8.0 - K.11.c.5.8.

The first objective was easily reached, and, after a pause of 42 minutes at the first protective barrage, the attack was resumed and the line established just short of the final objective. The final protective barrage for this line was provided by flank Artilleries owing to the conformation of the ground.

9.8.18. Batteries then moved forward to positions in and near K.26., West of MALARD WOOD, being in the following positions by dawn, 9th August, covering the front from K.10.a.0.0 to K.24.c.0.0. in case of counter-attack from the N.E. or N.

290th Bde. R.F.A.	J.36.c.
291st Bde. R.F.A.	K.26.a.
5th Army Bde. R.H.A.	K.31.a. and b. K.25.d.
86th Army Bde. R.F.A.	J.24.d. K.19.a.
250th Bde. R.F.A.	K.25.b. K.26.c.
251st Bde. R.F.A.	J.36.b. J.30.a.
18th Army Bde. R.F.A.	J.36.b.

At 5.30 p.m., August 9th, the attack was resumed by the 175th Infantry Brigade and the 131st Regiment American Infantry. The barrage opened on the line K.15.c.00.61 - K.35.c.60.50, the objective being the line K.24.d.1.5. - K.18.c.0.0. - K.17.cent. - K.11.c.3.0.(Railway) - K.11.a.1.4.(Road Junction

The Artillery covering this attack were the seven Brigades given above, the 12th Division co-operating on our left flank. The attack was successful and the gains were consolidated during the ensuing 24 hours.

10.8.18. On the night of the 10th, 5th Army Bde. R.H.A., 290th and 291st Brigades R.F.A. co-operated with the 4th Australian Division and cleared up the situation South of the above line and captured CHIPILLY and the spur to the North of it.

11.8.18. On the 11st inst., batteries moved forward to

290th Bde. R.F.A.	K.21.a. and c.
291st Bde. R.F.A.	K.27.b. K.28.a. K.22.d.
250th Bde. R.F.A.	K.23.a. and c.
251st Bde. R.F.A.	K.22.a., c., and d.
5th Army Bde. R.H.A.	K.22.a., c., and d.

12.8.18. The Infantry established themselves on a line East of

ETINHEM /

ETINHEM on the morning of the 12th.   They were shelled out of it but retook it the same night.

Batteries moved forward keeping close support with the Infantry and, when not on barrage work, fire was kept up on hostile tracks, approaches, river crossings, etc. from information from F.O.O.s, patrols, air reports and photographs. Harassing fire was carried out at night.

GENERAL.

Casualties during operations were exceptionally light, but, during a preliminary reconnaissance, 1 Brigade Commander, 2 Battery Commanders and 1 Captain were wounded, and 2 Battery Commanders killed near CHESSBOARD WOOD.   Batteries and Divisional Ammunition Column also suffered casualties to personnel and teams from shell fire and gas during the occupation of positions on the night 7th/8th August and while bringing up ammunition before that date.

Maxwell

A.D.A. 392

58th Division.

With reference to your GX. 212 of 12th inst., herewith Précis of Operations from 8th August to 12th August 1918.

Maxwell

15th August 1918.

Brigadier General,
C.R.A., 58th Division.

Appendix 'A'

PRÉCIS OF OPERATIONS
from 8th to 12th August 1918.

Reference Sheet 62.D.N.E. 1/20,000.

GENERAL PLAN.

The 50th and 58th Divisional Artilleries (under the command of C.R.A., 58th Division) and 86th Army Brigade R.F.A. covered the attack of the 58th Division on the front K.25.a.92.70 - J.36.c.0.0., with their first objective K.27.b.90.50 - K.27.d.90.00 - K.33.c.87.30 and final objective (approx.) Road running through K.22.a.00.75 - K.33.c.0.0 - K.29.a.5.5.

EXECUTION.

8.8.18.   Positions had been carefully reconnoitred in the Forward Area for this attack, but, owing to a German raid in the area selected on 6th August (in which 2 of our gunners were captured, of whom one afterwards escaped), these positions could not be occupied.

New positions were therefore selected at the last minute, batteries were moved up during the night and in position by midnight, 7th/8th August, as follows :-

290th Bde. R.F.A.	J.22.d. and J.28.c.
291st Bde. R.F.A.	J.28.b.
250th Bde. R.F.A.	J.16.d.
251st Bde. R.F.A.	J.22.b.
86th Army Bde. R.F.A.	J.23.c.

Forward Wagon Lines were established E. of the River ANCRE between BONNAY and HEILLY, for the replenishment of ammunition.

The Barrage opened at 4.20 a.m. on the 8th. The Infantry report that the barrage was good, and from the reports of F.O.O.s it appeared well-timed and even. Visibility was impossible during the early part of the morning owing to a think mist, which was favourable to our Infantry, prisoners stating that the attack was a complete surprise. There was hardly any reply to our barrage by the enemy Field Artillery and hostile Counter-battery work on our positions was nil. A smoke barrage was employed from /

2.

from Zero to Zero plus 4 hours on the line K.9.a.8.8 - K.10.a.8.0 - K.11.c.5.8.

The first objective was easily reached, and, after a pause of 42 minutes at the first protective barrage, the attack was resumed and the line established just short of the final objective. The final protective barrage for this line was provided by flank Artilleries owing to the conformation of the ground.

9.8.18. Batteries then moved forward to positions in and near K.26. West of MALARD WOOD, being in the following positions by dawn, 9th August, covering the front from K.10.a.0.0 to K.24.c.0.0. in case of counter-attack from the N.E. or N.

290th Bde. R.F.A.	J.36.c.
291st Bde. R.F.A.	K.26.a.
5th Army Bde. R.H.A.	K.31.a. and b. K.25.d.
26th Army Bde. R.F.A.	J.24.d. K.19.a.
250th Bde. R.F.A.	K.25.b. K.26.c.
251st Bde. R.F.A.	J.36.b. J.30.a.
18th Army Bde. R.F.A.	J.36.b.

At 5.30 p.m., August 9th, the attack was resumed by the 175th Infantry Brigade and the 131st Regiment American Infantry. The barrage opened on the line K.15.c.00.61 - K.35.c.60.50, the objective being the line K.24.d.1.5. - K.18.c.0.0. - K.17.cent. - K.11.c.3.0 (Railway) - K.11.a.1.4.(Road Junction)

The Artillery covering this attack were the seven Brigades given above, the 12th Division co-operating on our left flank. The attack was successful and the gains were consolidated during the ensuing 24 hours.

10.8.18. On the night of the 10th, 5th Army Bde. R.H.A., 290th and 291st Brigades R.F.A. co-operated with the 4th Australian Division and cleared up the situation South of the above line and captured CHIPILLY and the spur to the North of it.

11.8.18. On the 11st inst., batteries moved forward to

290th Bde. R.F.A.	K.21.a. and c.
291st Bde. R.F.A.	K.27.b. K.28.a. K.22.d.
250th Bde. R.F.A.	K.23.a. and c.
251st Bde. R.F.A.	K.22.a., c., and d.
5th Army Bde. R.H.A.	K.22.a., c., and d.

12.8.18. The Infantry established themselves on a line East of

ETINHEM on the morning of the 12th. They were shelled out of it but retook it the same night.

Batteries moved forward keeping close support with the Infantry and, when not on barrage work, fire was kept up on hostile tracks, approaches, river crossings, etc. from information from F.O.O.s, patrols, air reports and photographs. Harassing fire was carried out at night.

GENERAL.

Casualties during operations were exceptionally light, but, during a preliminary reconnaissance, 1 Brigade Commander, 2 Battery Commanders and 1 Captain were wounded, and 2 Battery Commanders killed near CHESSBOARD WOOD. Batteries and Divisional Ammunition Column also suffered casualties to personnel and teams from shell fire and gas during the occupation of positions on the night 7th/8th August and while bringing up ammunition before that date.

Maxwell
Brig General
CRA 58 Div

Appendix "B"

NARRATIVE OF EVENTS

from 25th August to 1st September 1918.

3 p.m. 25.8.18.   C.R.A., 58th Division, took over from C.R.A., 47th Division, when the position was as follows :-

Divisional Boundaries - South L.5.cent. - A.27.cent. thence East Grid Line.
North A.13.d.0.5. - A.16.a.0.5. - B.13.a.0.4. - B.14.cent. thence East Grid Line.

Our Infantry encountered strong M.G. opposition from BILLON WOOD and our Artillery Brigades, consisting of (North to South) 82nd, 86th, 104th, 251st, 150th, 250th Brigades, brought fire to bear and the enemy were eventually ejected.

150th Army Brigade R.F.A. was ordered to move forward and reconnoitre positions in F.23. to cover old German front line in A.23. and A.17. 104th Army Brigade R.F.A. was ordered to move forward to reconnoitred positions in F.29. to cover old German positions in A.23. and A.29.; to be in positions at 5 p.m.

4.35 p.m.   174th Infantry Brigade co-operating on right flank of 173rd Infy. Brigade had 250th and 150th (Army) Brigades R.F.A. placed at the disposal of the B.G.C., with headquarters at B.28.d.2.4. and F.21.d.8.0 respectively. B.G.C. 173rd Infy. Brigade had 86th and 104th Army Brigades R.F.A. (H.Q. at F.27.b.5.9. and F.28.b.9.8. respectively) placed at his disposal.

26.8.18.   The 173rd and 174th Infantry Brigades, having pushed out strong fighting patrols during the night, attacked the old German line in A.15.d., A.22.a. and c. and A.28.a. at 4.30 a.m. under cover of an Artillery barrage fired by 250th, 150th 104th and 86th Brigades R.F.A., the fire of 251st Brigade R.F.A. being superimposed over the whole front.

The situation at 9 a.m. was a follows :- General A.27.c. - A.27.a. - A.21.d. - Cross roads A.21.b.2.8. - thence to OXFORD COPSE - LAPREE WOOD, with posts pushed out in front at certain points.

251st/

2.

251st and 291st Brigades R.F.A. passed to 3rd Aust D.A. and 58th D.A. respectively at 12 noon. 291st Brigade were ordered to advance to more forward positions (L.4.a.6.7.)

At the conclusion of the day's fighting, the line ran approx. A.15.cent. Cross roads A.21.b.2.8. - A.22.c.0.0. - G.4.b.0.5.

A Location Statement giving the position of this D.A. Group at 6 p.m. is attached.

27.8.18. The attack on the enemy was continued at 4.55 a.m. in conjunction with 3rd Aust. and 12th Divisions on our right and left respectively under cover of an artillery barrage, the objectives being trench system in A.17.a. and c., A.23.a. and c. and A.29.a.

By 3 p.m. the whole Divisional Objective had been reached and MARICOURT clear of the enemy.

250th and 290th Brigades R.F.A. passed to 3rd Aust. D.A. and 58th D.A. respectively.

150th Army Brigade R.F.A. pulled out to Wagon Lines in K.17. in preparation for entrainment at LONGEAU on 30th August for another Army front.

Brigades again moved forward into positions in the neighbourhood of BILLON WOOD.

28.8.18. The attack was continued at 4.55 a.m. by 173rd and 174th Infy. Brigades under a barrage fired by 86th (H.Q. F.27.b.3.8.) 290th (H.Q. F.28.b.6.7.) 104th (H.Q. A.26.d.6.9.) and 291st (H.Q. F.30.c.3.0) Brigades R.F.A. from North to South, the final objective being the line A.18.b.0.5. - A.18.c.4.0 - A.30.a.0.0. being a very short advance, about 1000 yards.

At 10 p.m., under cover of an artillery barrage, posts were established in areas around A.13.c.0.0. and A.19.c.0.0.

H.Q.R.A. moved to L.1.b.3.0. at 3 p.m. A Location Statement of the Divisional Artillery Group at 6 p.m. is attached.

29.8.18.

3.

29.8.18. 175th Infantry Brigade established posts in RED FARM - B.19.a.
cent. - B.13.c.2.0 and patrols reported BATTERY COPSE unoccupied.
At 8.15 p.m. the 175th Infantry Brigade held the two trench
lines S.W. and S.E. of the South end of MAUREPAS, with patrols
pushed out in advance.

All Artillery Brigades advanced to positions in A.23. and A.30.

30.8.18. Orders were issued for the advance to be continued as rapidly
as possible with 175th Infantry Brigade and 3 R.F.A. Brigades
(86th 290th and 291st.) as advance guard. 104th Army Bde.R.F.A.
was ordered to remain in its same location in order to rest
personnel and horses, but to be ready to advance at shortest
notice if called upon.

Positions were taken up by the three forward Brigades in
B.22, 27, 28, and H.3. and 4, being in close proximity to the
Infantry Brigade Headquarters at B.26.b.7.0.

D.A.H.Q. closed at L.1.b.4.0. and reopened at A.19.b.6.2.
(CARNOY STATION).

The boundary between Australian Corps and III Corps, of
which 58th Division was Right Division, was amended slightly
temporarily to allow the former to carry out their operations
taking advantage of the terrain.

Sandford's Group of 60 pounders ceased to be attached to
the Division and reverted to Corps H.A. One section of
60 pounders of 144th Heavy Battery was placed at the disposal
of the Divisional Commander.

31.8.18. The attack was continued on MARRIERS WOOD, from which
M.G. fire had prevented our troops gaining their objective of
30th by about 500 yards, at 5.10 a.m., the line of the
Protective Barrage being C.14.c.5.0. - C.14.a.6.0., on which
fired was maintained for 5 minutes.

At 12 noon the Infantry were reported to be approximately
on their objective throughout, with posts pushed forward.

A Location Statement of the positions occupied by the

D.A.Group/

D.A. Group on the night 31st August/1st September is attached.

1.9.18, The attack was continued by 173rd Infantry Brigade., the barrage opening on line C.20.b.5.2. - C.20.b.0.4. - C.14.a.6.1. - and rested on a Protective Barrage on C.16.d.8.7. - C.17.a.2.5. - C.11.c.0.9. - C.10.b.5.2., and guns were again pushed forward in close support of Infantry.

At 4 p.m. C.R.A., 58th Division handed over the Artillery covering the 58th Divisional front to C.R.A., 74th Division.

2.9.18. The orders for the barrage, which included some smoke, to cover the attack of the 229th Infantry Brigade, 74th Division, with objectives D.10.c.0.0. - D.10.a.2.0. - D.4.c.0.0. - D.3.b.0.0. - D.2.b.0.0. were issued by C.R.A., 58th Division, and the Brigades were moved up in order to secure the maximum range possible. The locations of their Headquarters, which were in close proximity to their batteries in each case, were as follows :-

290th Brigade R.F.A.	B.30.b.6.4.
291st Brigade R.F.A.	B.30.b.9.8.
86th Army Bde. RFA.	B.23.c.2.5.
104th Army Bde. RFA.	B.29.d.0.8.

2 guns each of the above Brigades advanced with the Infantry and by close co-operation with the latter did very effective work on moving targets in the open.

The two Brigades R.F.A. of the 74th Divisional Artillery did not take part in the barrage but were kept on wheels ready to push forward to give the support necessary to the Infantry for the great advance contemplated. The command of the R.F.A. Brigades became vested in the B.G.C. 229th Infantry Brigade from Zero onwards.

Maxwell
Brig. General.
Commanding 58th Divisional Arty.

SECRET. Copy No. 14

58th Divisional Artillery Order No. 150.

5th August 1918.

Para. 1 is cancelled.

2.

4. Responsibility for Artillery Defence of the Divisional Sector from 10 a.m. August 6th.

250th Brigade R.F.A. and 251st Brigade R.F.A. will be responsible for the defence of the Divisional Sector from 10 a.m. August 6th until 5 p.m. August 7th.

10.30

~~Up to that hour, the batteries of JONES GROUP will be super-imposed over the whole Divisional front, but will not fire in case of S.O.S. except by order of these Headquarters.~~

10.30

From 5 p.m. August 7th until Zero hour, JONES GROUP will assume responsibility for the Artillery Defence of the Divisional Sector.

O.C., JONES GROUP, will arrange in consultation with B.G.C. 174th Infantry Brigade that, if possible, the more exposed batteries do not fire in answer to a S.O.S. Call.

5. **6" Newton Mortars.**

   1 Mortar 50th Divisional Artillery will remain in action at J.30.b.90.25.

   All remaining mortars in action will be withdrawn from action after dark August 7th.

   The surplus personnel of T.M. Batteries (50th and 58th Divisional Artilleries) will form a reserve of personnel available for special working parties on making tracks, filling in trenches, etc.

   Application for such working parties should be made to Staff Captain, 58th Divisional Artillery.

6. Tasks for 4.5" Howitzers and the one 6" Newton Mortar are shewn on Table "A" attached.

   After Zero plus 4 hours, D/251st Bde. R.F.A. will be prepared to advance. As soon as the situation permits, a position will be reconnoitred from which the ground in K.18. can be engaged.

   The barrage map for 18-pounders will be forwarded as soon as possible.

7. Liaison Officers (not below the rank of Captain) will be supplied to Infantry Brigades as follows :-
   JONES GROUP .... 174th Infy. Brigade
                              H.Q. J.22.d.2.3.
   SEDGWICKS GROUP .... 173rd Infy. Bde.
                              H.Q. J.28.a.8.9.

   Communication will be arranged for these Officers with both Groups and thence to the forward D.A.H.Q. in J.19.c.

   These Officers will report at the Headquarters of the Infantry Brigade to which they are attached at 9 a.m. August 7th. Each Officer will be accompanied by two telephonists. Rations for 48 hours to be taken. Names of officers selected to be reported to this Office.

8. 1 Section, A/290th Bde. R.F.A. will support 2/10th London Regiment, 175th Infantry Brigade, which has been detailed to mop up SAILLY LAURETTE and the Valley of the SOMME.

   This Section will be under the orders of the Battalion Commander from Zero until the conclusion of the operation.

   O.C., A/290th Bde. R.F.A. will arrange all details direct with O.C., 2/10th Bn. London Regiment (H.Q. 500 yds. North of VAUX sur SOMME)

Ammunition/

2. The Field Artillery available to support the attack of the 58th Division will consist of :-

   58th Divisional Artillery.
   50th Divisional Artillery.
   86th Army Brigade R.F.A.

   Of this, 50th Divisional Artillery is at present in action in defensive positions.
   The battle positions already chosen for batteries will be occupied as follows on the night 6th/7th August by
   290th Brigade R.F.A.
   291st Brigade R.F.A.
   86th Army Brigade R.F.A.;
   on the night 7th/8th August by
   250th Brigade R.F.A.
   251st Brigade R.F.A.

   Any casualties that occur to horses or vehicles during occupation of positions or dumping of ammunition must be cleared from road and either removed or camouflaged before dawn the following morning.

   On the night 7th/8th August, all batteries will form forward Wagon Lines. (Gun limbers, firing battery wagons, first line wagons and a proportion of outriders) These forward Wagon Lines will be East of the RIVER ANCRE between BONNAY and HEILLY. Brigades will be informed as to areas allotted.

3. The Artillery will be grouped when in action in the selected battle positions as under :-

   JONES GROUP.   (290th Bde. R.F.A.
   Lt. Col. W.A.F. JONES, D.S.O.   (291st Bde. R.F.A.
                                         (86th Army Bde. R.F.A.

   SEDGWICKS GROUP
   Lt. Col. F.R. SEDGWICK, D.S.O.   (250th Bde. R.F.A.
                                         (251st Bde. R.F.A.

   Location of Group Headquarters, which will be in J.22.c. and J.28.a. will be communicated to all concerned as soon as they are definitely settled.

4. Responsibility /

3.

Ammunition will be carried in the proportion of 50% A and 50% AX.

9. 1 Section, B/291st Bde. R.F.A. will be attached to the 173rd Infantry Brigade, which is the Brigade ordered to advance from the First Objective to capture the Final Objective.

This Section will come under the orders of B.G.C. 173rd Infy. Brigade as a temporary grouping from the time of leaving the First Objective to the capture of the Final Objective.

This Section will be in Mobile Reserve at Zero, East of the River ANCRE. A suitable place will be reconnoitred by O.C., B/291st Bde. R.F.A.

O.C., B/291st Bde. R.F.A. will get immediately into touch with B.G.C. 173rd Infy. Bde. and ascertain the probable role to be played by the Section.

The line of advance for the Section must be carefully reconnoitred, care being taken that the fire of the batteries firing on the barrage is not masked. O.C., B/291st Bde. R.F.A. should apply to 174th Infy. Brigade for any assistance he may require in bridging trenches, clearing gaps in the wire, etc., which can be carried out prior to the day of attack.

For filling in trenches and cutting gaps in the wire both before Zero and on the day of attack, D.T.M.O., 58th Division, will detail 1 N.C.O. and 12 men to report to O.C., B/291st Bde. R.F.A. (J.24.c.8.3.) at 6 a.m. August 7th.

O.C., B/291st Bde. R.F.A. will give all orders to this party and will supply it with picks, shovels and wire-cutters.

This party will rejoin its own unit on completion of this work.

All further details will be arranged between B.G.C. 173rd Infy. Bde. and O.C., B/291st Bde. R.F.A.

10. One dismounted Officers' Patrol will be pushed out by each Group on the day of attack as soon after Zero as the situation permits. Each patrol will collect and send back information as to the progress of the attack. The patrol from JONES GROUP will take the Southern half, that from SEDGWICKS GROUP the Northern half of the Divisional Sector. Both patrols will however, send back all information which they can obtain as to the situation on the Divisional Front and the progress of the attack on the front of flank Divisions.

Group Commanders will arrange the exact composition of patrols, and arrange communications with the rear with Captain Warrington, 58th Divisional Artillery Signals Officer.

11. O.C., JONES GROUP, will detail one Officer to supervise the Smoke Screen in K.9, K.10, K.11, as detailed in Table "A"

He will be stationed where he can best observe the effect of the fire and control the rate of fire.

12. Care will be taken that all batteries have as far as possible their establishment of telephone line.

13. All batteries will carry petrol tins filled with drinking water on their vehicles for supplying the personnel at the guns.

14. As the success of the operation depends upon its surprise effect, the greatest secrecy will be observed. All orders will only be communicated to those directly concerned.

No telephones or buzzers or any circuit in advance of batteries in positions that have not been before occupied will be /

be used before Zero.

Every precaution must be taken by batteries bringing guns into action in the battle positions to prevent disclosure of unusual activity.

On August 7th, O.C., JONES GROUP will detail an Officer to see that there is no movement/in the neighbourhood of the guns.

whatever

15. ACKNOWLEDGE.

Issued at 11.35 m.

Major,
A/Brigade Major, R.A.,
58th Divisional Artillery.

Distribution :-

290th Bde. R.F.A.	1.
291st Bde. R.F.A.	2.
86th Bde. R.F.A.	3.
D.T.M.O., 58th Division	4.
50th Div. Arty.	5.
250th Bde. R.F.A.	6.
251st Bde. R.F.A.	7.
D.T.M.O., 50th Division.	8.
18th Div. Arty.	9.
R.A., IIIrd Corps	10.
H.A., IIIrd Corps	11.
Staff Captain, R.A.	12.
Signals Officer R.A.	13.
58th Division "G"	14.
173rd Infy. Bde.	15.
174th Infy. Bde.	16.
175th Infy. Bde.	17.
R.O., R.A.	18.

Table "A"
(58th D.A. Order No. 150)

4.5" HOWITZER BARRAGE.

Battery.	Times.	Tasks.	Rates of fire.
D/290 D/291	Zero to Zero plus 4 mins.	Bombard SAILLY LAURETTE and Valley in area :- K.31.c.2.7. - K.31.a.8.3. - K.31.b.5.7. - K.31.c.6.5.	INTENSE.
ditto	Zero plus 4 mins to Zero plus 10 mins.	SAILLY LAURETTE S. and E. of line J.36.d.5.0 - J.36.d.5.2. - K.31.c.5.5.	RAPID.
ditto	Zero plus 10 mins to Zero plus 20 mins.	Bombard Valley in Area K.32.b.o.6- K.32.b.6.8. - K.27.c.4.0. - K.27.d.0.7. - K.33.c.8.5.7. - K.33.a.0.0.	First 5 mins. NORMAL. Last 5 mins. RAPID.
ditto	Zero plus 20 mins to Zero plus 128 mins.	Bombard Valley in Area K.34.c.2.0- K.34.a.5.5. - K.28.d.0.1 - K.34.c.7.0	First 40 mins. SLOW Next 10 mins. RAPID. Last 58 mins. SLOW.
ditto	Zero plus 128 mins. to Zero plus 135 mins.	Bombard Valley in area K.34.c.2.0- K.34.c.3.4. - K.34.a.9.3. - K.34.c.7.0	First 2 mins. SLOW. Last 5 mins. RAPID.
Ammunition BX.		As many 106 fuzes as possible will be used.	

S M O K E   S C R E E N.

D/250 D/251	Zero to Zero plus 4 hours.	K.9.a.8.8. - K.10.a.8.0	First 4 mins. INTENSE. Next 26 mins. NORMAL. Last 210 mins. SLOW. or as ordered by officer specially detailed to supervise this screen.
D/86		K.10.a.8.0 - K.11.c.5.8.	

The proportion of gas to be used in this Smoke Screen will be notified later.

P.T.O.

Table "A" Contd.

6" Newton Mortar will bombard SAILLY LAURETTE VILLAGE at a Rapid rate from Zero to Zero plus 15 mins.

In case our Infantry are checked and further bombardment of the Village is required, D.T.M.O., 50th Division, will detail one Officer to get into touch with O.C., 2/10th Bn. London Regiment (H.Q. 500 yards North of VAUX-sur-SOMME) by midday 7th inst. This Officer will accompany the Battalion Commander on the day of attack and must make arrangements so that he can repeat the bombardment with the 6" Newton Mortar, should the Battalion Commander desire it.

SECRET.

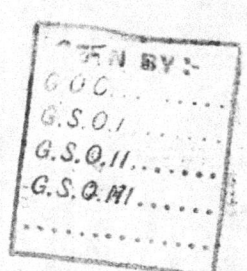 

Amendment No. 1 to 58th D.A. Order No. 150.

1. (a) Para. 4, line 5, delete "5 p.m." and substitute "10.30 p.m."

   (b) Delete para. "Up to that hour .... Headquarters".

   (c) Line 9, delete "5 p.m." and substitute "10.30 p.m."

2. Table "A" Smoke Screen.

   For "K.9.a.8.8." substitute "K.9.b.8.8."

Major,
A/Brigade Major, R.A.,
58th Divisional Artillery.

6th August 1918.

To all recipients of 58th D.A. Order No. 150.

SECRET.

Amendment No. 3 to 58th D.A. Order No. 150.

Table "A".

1. In column of "TIMES"

   Para. 3, line 2, for "Zero plus 20 minutes" read "Zero plus 40 minutes".

   Para. 4, line 1, for "Zero plus 20 minutes" read "Zero plus 40 minutes".

2. In column of "Rates of Fire".

   Para. 3, line 1, for "First 5 minutes" read "First 25 minutes".

   Para. 4, line 1, for "First 40 minutes" read "First 20 minutes".

3. ACKNOWLEDGE.

(signed)

Major,
A/Brigade Major, R.A.,
58th Divisional Artillery.

7th August 1918.

To All recipients of 58th D.A. Order No. 150.

36 Div. | 18 Div.

J | K
   31

Ref Sheet
62D.NE
Scale 1:20000

INF. START LINE

FIRST OBJECTIVE

FINAL OBJECTIVE

K
36

SECRET   Copy No. 14

58th Divisional Artillery Order No. 151.

6th August 1918.

Reference 58th D.A. Order No. 150 and Maps Sheets 62^D N.E. and S.E., 1/20,000.

1. At Zero hour, which will be notified later, all guns and howitzers detailed to take part in the operation will open fire.
    Harassing fire, which must be no less than usual, will be carried out on the night preceding the attack. Further orders will be issued on this subject.

2. The attack will be covered by a creeping barrage (see attached tracing) which will precede the Infantry and Tanks.
    At Zero it will be formed on a line 300 yards beyond the forming up line of the Infantry.
    The first lift will be at Zero plus 4. The barrage will creep by lifts of 100 yards at a time and will conform to the lines and times on attached tracing.
    The numbers against each line give the time at which the barrage will lift from the line in question.
    At Zero plus 115, 86th Army Brigade R.F.A. passes to the command of the 18th Divisional Artillery.
    At Zero plus 110, Brigades will adjust their fire so as to cover their new zones on the protective barrage for the first objective.

    Rates of Fire.

    First 4 minutes. .... Intense.
    First 4 minutes after leaving
      Protective Barrage for First
      Objective .... Intense.
    Remainder of Creeping Barrage ... Normal.

3. Protective Barrage.

    For the First Objective.
    On reaching the Proective Barrage Line, each battery will remain stationary for 20 minutes, after which it will search to a depth of 500 yards once in every 10 minutes.
    Fire on the Proective Barrage will be continued in the intervals between the bursts of searching fire.

    For the Final Objective, there will be no Protective Barrage on this Divisional Sector, owing to the conformation of the ground. Orders as to S.O.S. Lines will be issued later.

    Batteries will cease firing on the barrage line at the time marked against the most Easterly barrage line in their particular zone.

    Rates of Fire.
    18-pounders.

    During Searching .... NORMAL.
    From 15 minutes before the Protective
      Barrage for the First Objective is timed
      to lift to 12 minutes before this time .. INTENSE.
    Remaining 12 minutes of this barrage .... NORMAL.

4. AMMUNITION.

4. **AMMUNITION.**

18-pounders will fire Shrapnel at ranges up to 5000 yards, 50% on graze
   Care will be taken that sufficient 106 fuzes are retained for use with H.E. at long ranges.
   If the weather is wet, every 18-pounder will fire one round of smoke shell in every 15 rounds.

5. **Light Signals.**

The following Light Signals will be employed by the IIIrd Corps :-
   (a) GREEN over GREEN over GREEN   meaning   S.O.S.
   (b) WHITE over WHITE over WHITE   ....   Success Signal, i.e. We have reached Objective.
   (c) 1 WHITE VERY LIGHT meaning "Barrage is about to lift"

6. **Calls from the Air.**

   (1) During the Barrage.

One battery per Brigade will be detailed to answer calls from the air during the barrage. These batteries will be superimposed on the barrage.
   The only calls that will be answered by these batteries will be
   (a) LL Calls.   These will be answered by three salvoes immediately on receipt of the call. If the call is repeated after a reasonable interval, the bursts will be fired again.
   (b) LLNF.   These calls will be used to bring fire to bear on anti-tank guns. Procedure will be as for "LL" Calls.
   (c) S.O.S.   This call will be answered by firing for 5 minutes at an intense rate on the threatened area, followed by 5 minutes at rapid rate. The fire will then be slowed down if the situation permits, and the battery will return to its barrage programme.

   (2) After the completion of the Barrage Programme.
   (a) "GF" Calls will be answered by a Section of all batteries that can bring fire to bear.
   (b) "LL" Calls will be answered by all batteries that can bring fire to bear on the target with the exception of one 18-pounder battery of each Brigade which will remain covering the zone allotted to the Brigade.

In both cases, the call will be answered by 3 salvoes. This will be repeated, if the call is repeated after a reasonable interval.

7. **Tank Signals.**

The following signals will be used between tanks and Infantry :-
   (1) From Infantry to Tanks.
       A steel helmet raised on a fixed bayonet denotes "Tank assistance required".

   (2) /

3.

 (2) From Tanks to Infantry.
   Green and White Flag denotes "Come on".
   Red and Yellow Flag denotes   "Out of Action".
   Tricolour Flag denotes   "Coming back".

8. Acknowledge.

                 Major,
              A/Brigade Major, R.A.
Issued at 3.30 p.m.   58th Divisional Artillery.

 Distribution :-

  290th Bde. R.F.A.   1.
  291st Bde. R.F.A.   2
  86th Bde. R.F.A.   3
  D.T.M.O., 58th Division 4.
  50th Div. Arty.   5
  250th Bde. R.F.A.   6
  251st Bde. R.F.A.   7
  D.T.M.O., 50th Div. 8
  18th Div. Arty.   9
  R.A., IIIrd Corps   10
  H.A., IIIrd Corps   11
  Staff Captain R.A.   12
  Signals Officer R.A. 13
  58th Division "G"   14
  173rd Infy. Bde.   15
  174th Infy. Bde.   16
  175th Infy. Bde.   17
  R.O.R.A.   18

Identification Trace for use with Artillery Maps.

SECRET.   Copy No. 6

58th Divisional Artillery Order No.153.

Ref. Sheet 62d.N.E. 1/20,000.

1. The attack on the enemy defensive organisation will be continued on August 9th.
   Objectives are shewn on attached tracing "A".
   The attack will be covered by a creeping barrage of 18 pdrs. as shewn on Tracing "A", which also gives the zones allotted to the different groups. The 4.5" Hows will conform with the 18-pdr. barrage, keeping always 100^x in front of it and searching as far as possible such localities as are most likely to harbour the enemy. All lifts will be at the rate of 200^x every 8 minutes.

2. Rates of fire -

   0. 0. - 0.4.   Intense.
   1.40. - 1.45.   Intense.
   1.58. - 2. 2.   Intense.
   Remainder.   Normal.

   Ammunition -
   18-pdrs. will fire shrapnel at all ranges, up to 5000 yards with a corrector giving 60% on graze. Above this range H.E. will be used with 106 fuze. Smoke Shell will be fired at the rate of 1 round in every 15 for all barrages, provided the supply of ammunition ensures the full amount for protective barrages.

3. Group Commanders will push out officers patrol as usual to get into touch with the situation as it develops.

4. Co-operation with the R.A.F. and all necessary arrangements for it will be the same as for the operation carried out on August 8th.

5. III Corps Heavy Artillery are co-operating by bombarding hostile occupied areas and with counter-battery work.

6. Zero hour will be notified separately to those concerned.

7. ACKNOWLEDGE.

                                        Major,
                                        Brigade Major, R.A.
9th August 1918.   58th Divisional Artillery.

Copies to:-   Copy No.
JONES GROUP.   1.
SEDGWICKS GROUP.   2.
5th Army Bde. RHA.   3.
18th Army Bde. RFA.   4.
83rd Bde RFA.   5.
58th Div. G.   6.
III Corps R.A.   7.
III Corps H.A.   8.
4th Aust. D.A.   9.
18th D.A.   10.
25th D.A.   11.
131st Regt. American Inf. 12.
175th Infantry Bde.   13.

B.M./Y/424.

Reference 58th D.A. Order No. 153. -

Zero hour will be 5.30 a.m, 9th August.

Acknowledge.

9th August 1918.   *[signature]*
                                    Major,
                              for. Brigade Major, R.A.
                                58th Divisional Artillery.

G.S.G.S. 2021.

NOTE.—(1) These traces are intended to facilitate the communication of information as to the position of targets, which have been located on a squared map on the 1/40,000 scale.
(2) The squares on this trace are 500 yards in length on the 1/10,000 scale, 1,000 yards in length on the 1/20,000 scale, and 2,000 yards in length can be used for the 1/10,000, 1/20,000, or 1/40,000 scale.
(3) The squares on this tracer are fitted to the squares of the imperial, which are then drawn on the trace. Sufficient letters and numbers must also be added to enable the recipient to place the trace in the correct position on his own map. A little detail may also be traced, but this is not essential. The name and scale of the map referred to which the trace refers must be always given. The trace

Tracing taken from Sheet

of the 1: map of

Signature   Date

Identification Trace for use with Artillery Maps

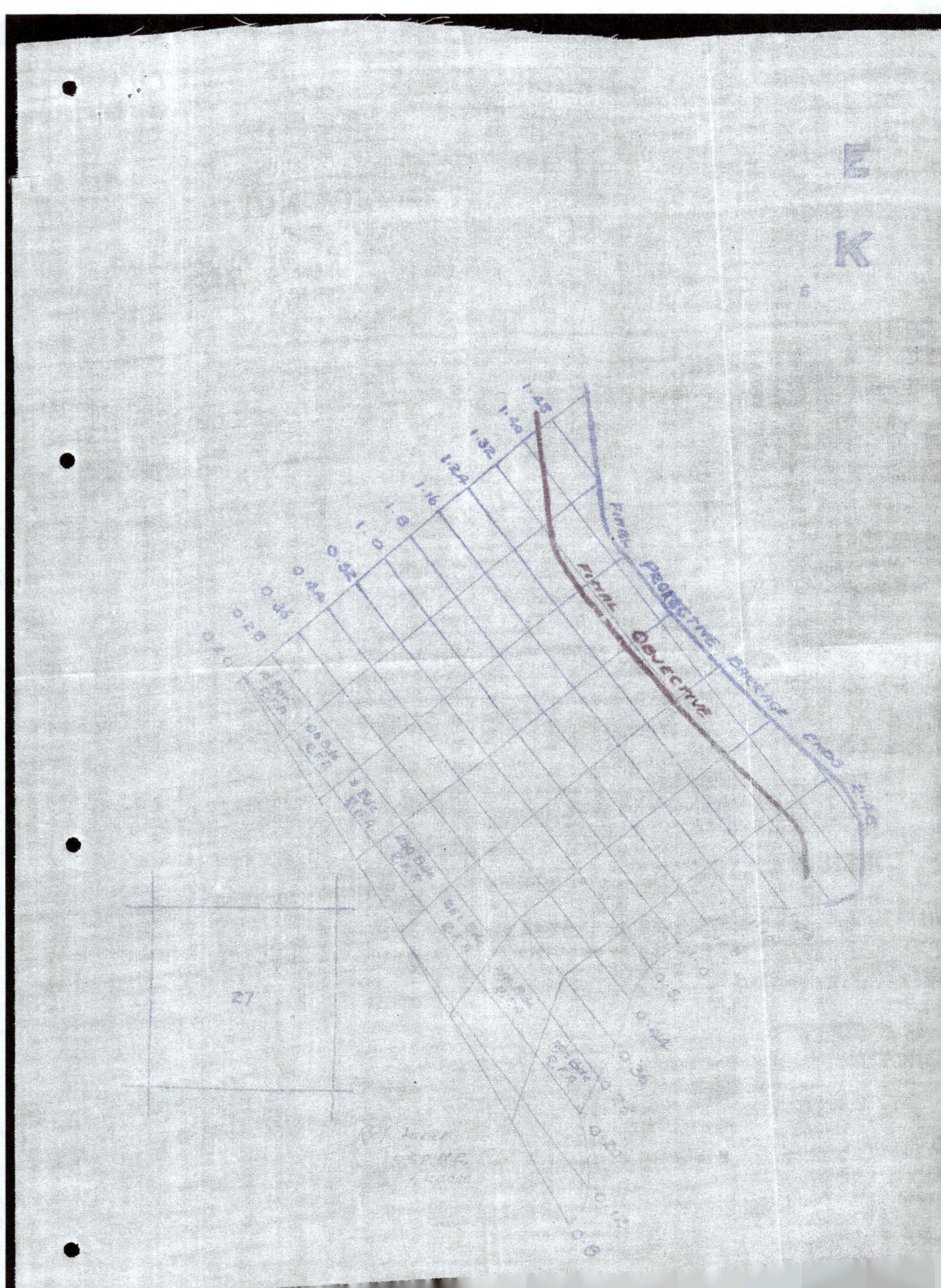

SECRET.   Copy No. 7

58th Divisional Artillery Order No.154.

1. The 175th Infantry Brigade and 131st American Infantry Regiment will attack this afternoon and capture the objectives shewn on attached tracing "A".
   The 12th Division are attacking on the left.

2. Details of the barrage covering the attack will be as detailed in 58th D.A.Order No.153, para 1. and as shewn on Tracing "A" attached hereto which cancels all previous issues.

3. From zero hour onwards the 5th Army Brigade RHA, 18th Army Brigade R.F.A. and 86th Army Brigade RFA come under the orders of C.R.A., 58th Division and the Final Protective Barrage will be the S.O.S. Line for troops under command of G.O.C., 58th Division, till further orders.

4. Ammunition as in 58th D.A. Order No.153.

   Rates of Fire.
   0.0. - 0.4.   Intense.
   Remainder.   Normal.

5. The Brigades mentioned in para.3 will send orderlies to these Headquarters at J.19.c.5.5. at once.

6. Zero hour will be 5.0 P.M.

7. ACKNOWLEDGE.

                                    H. Williams
                                    Major,
                                    Brigade Major R.A.
                                    58th Divisional Artillery.

9th August 1918.

Copies to:-   Copy No.
JONES GROUP,   1. (10)
SEDGWICKS GROUP.   2. (10)
5th Army Bde. RHA.   3. (5)
18th Army Bde. RFA.   4. (5)
86th Army Bde. RFA.   5. (5)
58th Div. "G"   6.
III Corps R.A.   7.
III Corps H.A.   8.
4th Aust. D.A.   9.
18th D.A.   10.
25th D.A.   11.
131st Regt. American Inf.   12.
175th Infantry Bde.   13.

SECRET.   Copy No. ....

58th Divisional Artillery Order No. 155.

1. 173rd and 174th Infantry Brigades are pushing forward strong Fighting Patrols during the night, followed by formed bodies of troops.
    At 4.30 a.m., they will endeavour to occupy the old German line in A.15.d., A.22.a. and c. and A.28.a.

2. 58th Divisional Artillery Group will co-operate as follows:-

    At 4.0 a.m.   All available 18-pounders and 4.5" Hows. open on the following line in their Brigade Zones -
    A.27.d.8.7. - A.28.a.4.9 - through trench in A.22.c. - A.22.a.8.2. - A.22.a.8.4. - A.21.b.9.5. - A.15.d.8.2. - A.15.d.3.4. - A.15.b.4.9.
                                       and remain till   4.30 a.m.

    At 4.30 a.m.   They lift to a line 300 yards beyond the above line and remain searching to a depth of 500 yards beyond it till   4.45 a.m.

    At 4.45 a.m.   STOP and all further orders for direction of fire will be received direct through Brigade H.Q. in consultation with B.G.s C. Infy. Bdes.

3. Rates of Fire.
    4.25 a.m. - 4.30 a.m. and 4.40 a.m. - 4.45 a.m.   INTENSE.
    Remainder of the time.   As fast as the ammunition situation will permit, at the discretion of Brigade Commanders.

4. Heavy Artillery are co-operating by bombarding MARICOURT and trench system in A.22. and A.29.a., within the limits of safety, timing their lifts in accordance with the Field Artillery barrage.

5. Artillery Brigades' fire will be superimposed over the whole front of the Infantry Brigades which they cover.

6. 251st Brigade R.F.A. will distribute its fire over the whole of the Divisional Front.

7. Artillery Brigades to acknowledge by wire.

                                           H. Williamson
                                                Major,
                                           Brigade Major, R.A.,
25th August 1918.   58th Divisional Artillery.

Copies to.
    250th Bde. R.F.A.   173rd Infy. Bde.
    251st Bde. R.F.A.   174th Infy. Bde.
    150th Bde. R.F.A.   58th Division "G"
    104th Bde. R.F.A.   R.A., III Corps.
    86th Bde. R.F.A.   L.O., H.A.
                         Sandford's H.A. Group

SECRET.   Copy No. 6

58th Divisional Artillery Order No.156.

1. The following alterations in the disposition of the Artillery covering the 58th Division front will take place and completion reported before 12 midnight August 27/28th.

    (a) 290th Brigade R.F.A. will relieve 150th Army Brigade R.F.A. in action but will cover the Left (at present 173) Infantry Brigade.
    All necessary information will be obtained from O.C., 86th Army Brigade R.F.A. with whom O.C., 290th Brigade R.F.A. will keep in continuous touch, and who will have a direct call upon his brigades

    (b) 150th Army Brigade R.F.A. on relief will withdraw to its wagon lines, prior to proceeding to a new area, under orders which will be issued later.

    (c) 250th Brigade R.F.A. will pass to the command of C.R.A., 3rd Australian Div. Arty

    (d) 291st Brigade R.F.A. will take over the defence of the front held by the Right (at present 174th) Infantry Brigade. The O.C., 291st Brigade R.F.A. will take over the H.Q. of O.C., 250th Brigade R.F.A., from whom he will receive all the necessary information and instructions; he will then be directly under the command of the B.G.C., Right Infantry Brigade.

    (e) O.C., 104th Army Brigade R.F.A. will connect up with H.Q., 291st Brigade R.F.A. and will take over the defence of the Right Brigade front; receiving all the necessary instructions and information from O.C., 291st Brigade R.F.A., who will have a direct call upon him.

2. The actual times and details of changing over commands will be arranged between the unit commander concerned, but they must ensure that one complete artillery brigade is always covering each Infantry Brigade front continuously.

3. A Location Statement is attached for the information of those concerned.

4.   ACKNOWLEDGE.

                                                H Williamson
                                                      Major,
                                            Brigade Major, R.A.
26th August 1918.   58th Divisional Artillery.

Copies to:-   Copy No
104th Army Bde. RFA.   1.
86th Army Bde. RFA.   2.
250th Brigade RFA.   3.
150th Army Bde. RFA.   4.
291st Brigade RFA.   5.
58th Division "G".   6.
R.A., III Corps.   7.
H.A., III Corps.   8.
173rd Infantry Brigade.   9.
174th Infantry Brigade.   10.
3rd Aust. D.A.   11.
290th Brigade R.F.A.   12.
Major Sandford's Group.   13.
71st Brigade R.G.A.   14.
27th Brigade R.G.A.   15.

SECRET. Copy No. 9

58th Divisional Artillery Group Order No. 157.

1. The 3rd Australian, 58th and 12th Divisions are attacking the Huns in their old Trench System on August 27th.

2. The objectives and lines for 18-pounders barrage fire, with Zones allotted to the Artillery Brigades, are shewn on attached tracing.

3. 4.5" Howitzers conform to 18-pounder barrage lines, keeping 100 yards East throughout.
   H.A. will co-operate in a similar way, keeping at a safe distance East of the 18-pounder barrage lines.
   Areas containing hostile batteries reported active on August 26th will be kept under fire by the 60-pounders of Major Sandford's Group.
   Remaining Heavy Artillery available will bombard areas selected from their own Intelligence Reports.

4. From Zero plus 2 hours till Zero plus 2.30 hours, the area between the Protective Barrage and the GREEN LINE, up to which the Infantry hope eventually to exploit, will be searched backwards and forwards.

5. At Zero plus 2.30 hours, control of the Artillery Brigades reverts to the B.G.s C. Infantry Brigade to which they are allotted. 291st Brigade R.F.A. comes again directly under C.R.A., 58th Division, superimposed over whole front.

6. Rates of Fire, for Field Artillery.

   0.15 - 0.20   Intense.
   Otherwise   Normal.

7. ZERO HOUR will be 4.55 a.m.

8. ACKNOWLEDGE.

H. Williams
Major,
Brigade Major, R.A.,
58th Divisional Artyl Group.

26th August 1918.

86th Army Bde. R.F.A.	1
104th Army Bde. R.F.A.	2
150th Army Bde. R.F.A.	3
250th Bde. R.F.A.	4
291st Bde. R.F.A.	5
Sandford's Group	6
71st Bde. R.G.A.	7
27th Bde. R.G.A.	8
58th Division	9
173rd Infy. Bde.	10
174th Infy. Bde.	11
175th Infy. Bde.	12
3rd Aust. D.A.	13
12th D.A.	14
R.A., IIIrd Corps	15
H.A., IIIrd Corps	16

S x 152
27/8/18.

A.D.A. 427.

Bde. R.F.A.

The G.O.C.R.A., IIIrd Corps, wishes it to be again impressed on Brigade and Battery Commanders that, during moving warfare such as is now in progress, individual enterprise must be given the fullest play.

Every Artillery Unit's role is to cover the advance of the Infantry on its own front and the best way to do this is to continually seek out and engage all or any hostile elements which are barring its progress.

Constant patrolling must be maintained by Officers from each Battery; otherwise it will not be possible to keep in sufficiently close touch with local situations. Brigades and Batteries will constantly have to change positions and forward wagon lines must be kept as close as possible to enable them to do this quickly.

All reconnaissances must be made mounted. Officers do not <u>yet</u> make sufficient use of their horses for this purpose.

There is a general tendency on the part of all ranks "<u>to await orders from Headquarters</u>"; this must be done away with. Owing to the difficulty of maintaining communications when units are on the move, decentralisation from D.A.H.Q. must be practised.

Whenever possible, the individual action of Brigades, when changes of positions are involved, should be reported to D.A.H.Q. as early as possible; also the arrangements made with the concurrence of the Infantry for the protection of the front.

Major,
Brigade Major, R.A.,
58th Divisional Artillery.

27th August 1918.

Copies to   58th Division "G"
            173rd Infy. Bde.
            174th Infy. Bde.
            175th Infy. Bde.

SECRET.   Copy No. 8

58th Divisional Artillery Order No. 158.

1. The enemy are now reported as holding their old front line trenches in A.17. 23. and 29.
    They will be attacked tomorrow morning, 28th August, by 173rd and 174th Infantry Brigades.

2. A Tracing is attached shewing objectives and the lines upon which 18-pounder barrage is to fall. The zones allotted to the Artillery Brigades are also shewn.

3. The 4.5" Hows. conform to the 18-pounder barrage keeping 100^x E. of it throughout.
    The IIIrd Corps H.A. will co-operate in a similar manner concentrating on trench junctions and suspected strong points in the old German system and always keeping a safe distance E. of the 18-pounder barrage according to the nature of the pieces employed.

4. Areas containing hostile batteries reported active on August 27th or the most Easterly ones reported on August 26th will be engaged by the 60-pounders of Major Sandford's Group, and any other Heavy Artillery which the Brigade Commanders can allot for the purpose without cutting down the bombardment programme.

5. From the time when the fire of each gun rests on the line of the Protective Barrage till Zero plus 1.42, the gun will search the area lying between the Protective Barrage line and the Line of Exploitation.

6. At Zero plus 1.42, the Field Artillery Brigades will revert to their normal zones as for before the operation, and tasks will be allotted to them by the B.G.s C. Infantry Brigades to which they are attached. All fire on the area between the Protective Barrage Line and the Line of Exploitation will cease at that hour unless otherwise ordered by them.

7. Rates of Fire.
    0.0 - 0.6   INTENSE.
    Remainder.   NORMAL.

8. Zero hour will be 4.55 a.m.

9. ACKNOWLEDGE.

                                                H. Williamson
                                                Major,
                                                Brigade Major, R.A.,
27th August 1918.   58th Divisional Artillery.

Copies to :-
290th Brigade R.F.A.	1.
291st Brigade R.F.A.	2.
104th Army Bde. R.F.A.	3
86th Army Bde. R.F.A.	4
Sandford's Group	5
71st Bde. R.G.A.	6
27th Bde. R.G.A.	7.
58th Division	8
173rd Infy Bde.	9
174th Infy. Bde.	10
175th Infy. Bde.	11
3rd Aust. D.A.	12
25th D.A.	13
R.A., IIIrd Corps	14
H.A., IIIrd Corps	15

LINE of EXPLOITATION

ENDS 1·42
1·36
1·30
1·24
1·18   PROTECTOR
1·12
1·0
0·54
0·8   FINAL OBJECTIVE
0·40
0·42
0·36
0·30
0·24
0·18
0·12   0·12
0·0
    86   290   104   291

Ref. Sheet 62 N.W.
Issued with O.A.
Order No 158

SECRET.   Copy No. 8

58th Divisional Artillery Order No. 159.

1. Artillery redistribution as from 12 noon, August 28th, will be as follows :-
   (a) Under direct orders of B.G.C. 173rd (Left) Infy. Bde.
       86th Army Bde. R.F.A.
       covering the front held by this Infantry Brigade as detailed in R.N. 71 dated 27th (addressed those concerned only)
   (b) Under direct orders of B.G.C. 174th (Right) Infy. Bde.
       291st Bde. R.F.A. and 104th Army Bde. R.F.A., on which O.C., 291st Bde. R.F.A. will have a direct call and to which he will transmit the requirements of B.G.C. Infantry Brigade.
       Distribution of the fire of these Brigades for S.O.S. purposes will be arranged by O.C., 291st Bde. R.F.A. and will cover the front held by this Infantry Brigade as detailed in R.N. 71.
   (c) Directly under the orders of C.R.A., 58th Division
       290th Brigade R.F.A. which will superimpose its fire over the whole Divisional Front as directed from D.A.H.Q.

2. All Artillery Brigades mentioned above will be dealt with direct from these Headquarters in matters affecting the whole Divisional Front, but for local movements and bombardments, their C.O.s will receive all necessary instructions from the B.Gs C. Infantry Brigade to which they are allotted, notifying D.A.H.Q. when possible of the action which they have taken, especially when it involves a move of Headquarters.

3. The 290th Brigade R.F.A. may be specially employed for operations not connected with the defence of the front, and the assistance of its fire must not be relied on at any time by the Officers Commanding the other Brigades.

4. Each Brigade must have at least one direct line to the Advanced Exchange and one mounted orderly must be kept as before at H.Q., 58th D.A., now at K.14.b.2.2. and moving tomorrow to L.1.b.2.0.
   These orderlies must have their rations and forage and, on any move of Brigade Headquarters taking place, a fresh orderly will be sent from Rear Headquarters with Brigade locations. The old orderly will then be returned.

5. Pending further instructions, O.C., 290th Brigade R.F.A. will distribute his fire for S.O.S. purposes as follows :-
   2 18-pdr. batteries   on Right Brigade Front.
   1 18-pdr. battery   on Left Brigade Front.
   1 4.5" How. Battery   Enfilading road in B.25.b.

6. Calls from the air will be answered by 1-18-pdr. Battery and 1 4.5" How. Section detailed for this purpose from each Brigade and in all defensive arrangements the fire of these batteries should be superimposed on that of the others so as to avoid leaving a gap in the barrage.

7. ACKNOWLEDGE.

                                              H Williamson
                                              Major,
                                              Brigade Major, R.A.,
                                              58th Divisional Artillery.

27th August 1918.

Distribution overleaf.

Distribution.   Copy No.

290th Brigade R.F.A.   1.
291st Brigade R.F.A.   2.
104th Army Brigade RFA.   3.
86th Army Brigade RFA.   4.
Sandford's Group.   5.
71st Brigade R.G.A.   6.
27th Brigade R.G.A.   7.
58th Division.   8.
173rd Infantry Brigade.   9.
174th Infantry Brigade.   10.
175th Infantry Brigade.   11.
3rd Aust. D.A.   12.
25th D....   13.
R.A., III Corps.   14.
H.A., III Corps.   15.
Signals, 58th Division.   16.
R.A., Signals Officer.   17.

SECRET.   Copy No. 8

58th Divisional Artillery Order No. 160.

1. 175th Infantry Brigade is taking over the line from 173rd and 174th Infantry Brigades tonight.   Their H.Q. will be A.20.b.1.2.
   86th Army, 104th Army, and 291st Brigades R.F.A. are placed at the disposal of B.G.C. 175th Infantry Brigade and will connect up to his Headquarters immediately.
   86th Army Brigade R.F.A. will be responsible for Liaison with Infantry Brigade H.Q. and B.G.C., 175th Infantry Brigade will ask for Battalion Liaison Officers direct from his allotted Artillery Brigades as required.   Zones allotted are divided by E. and W. grid lines passing through the following points :-
   291st Bde. R.F.A.   B.25.a.0.0.   and   B.19.c.0.4.
   104th Army Bde. R.F.A. B.19.c.0.4.   and   B.19.a.0.8.
   86th Army Bde. R.F.A. B.19.a.0.8.   and   B.13.a.0.4.

   The usual overlap will be provided.

2. For S.O.S. purposes, 290th Brigade R.F.A. will superimpose the fire of one of its batteries over that of each of the above Brigades and will concentrate its 4.5" Howitzers on M.G. Nest at A.24.b.4.3.

3. ACKNOWLEDGE.
   done

H.C. Williamson
Major,
Brigade Major, R.A.,
58th Divisional Artillery.

28th August 1918.

86th Army Bde. R.F.A.	1.
104th Army Bde. R.F.A.	2
290th Bde. R.F.A.	3
291st Bde. R.F.A.	4
Sandford's Group	5
71st Bde. R.G.A.	6
27th Bde. R.G.A.	7
58th Division	8
173rd Infy. Bde.	9
174th Infy. Bde.	10
175th Infy. Bde.	11
R.A., IIIrd Corps	12
H.A., IIIrd Corps	13
3rd Aust. D.A.	14
25th D.A.	15

SECRET. Amdt Copy No. 8

58th Divisional Artillery Order No. 161.

1. The 175th Infantry Brigade are endeavouring to establish posts in areas marked RED on attached tracing.

   Artillery support will be as follows :-

   0.0 - 0.15   Heavy Artillery bombard area enclosed within lines ABCD.

   0.15   Heavy Artillery stop and Field Artillery open fire with all guns and Hows. that can bear on line "AB" and remain till 0.21

   0.21   Lift 100^x and continue so doing every 6 minutes till line "CD" is reached on which they remain for 6 minutes and then STOP.

   Rates of Fire.   0.0 - 0.6   INTENSE.
                    REMAINDER   NORMAL.

2. S.O.S. Lines on completion of operation will be detailed by B.G.C. 175th Infantry Brigade as required.

3. Zero Hour will be 10.0 p.m., tonight, August 28th.

4. Watches will be synchronised under Group arrangements with H.Q., 175th Infantry Brigade.

5. ACKNOWLEDGE.

                                                    Major,
                                        Brigade Major, R.A.,
                                    58th Divisional Artillery.

28th August 1918.

Copies to
   86th Bde. R.F.A.
   104th Bde. R.F.A.
   290th Bde. R.F.A.
   291st Bde. R.F.A.
   Sandford's Group
   71st Bde. R.G.A.
   27th Bde. R.G.A.
   58th Division "G"
   173rd Infy. Bde.
   174th Infy. Bde.
   175th Infy. Bde.
   3rd Aust. D.A.
   25th D.A.
   R.A., IIIrd Corps.
   H.A., IIIrd Corps.

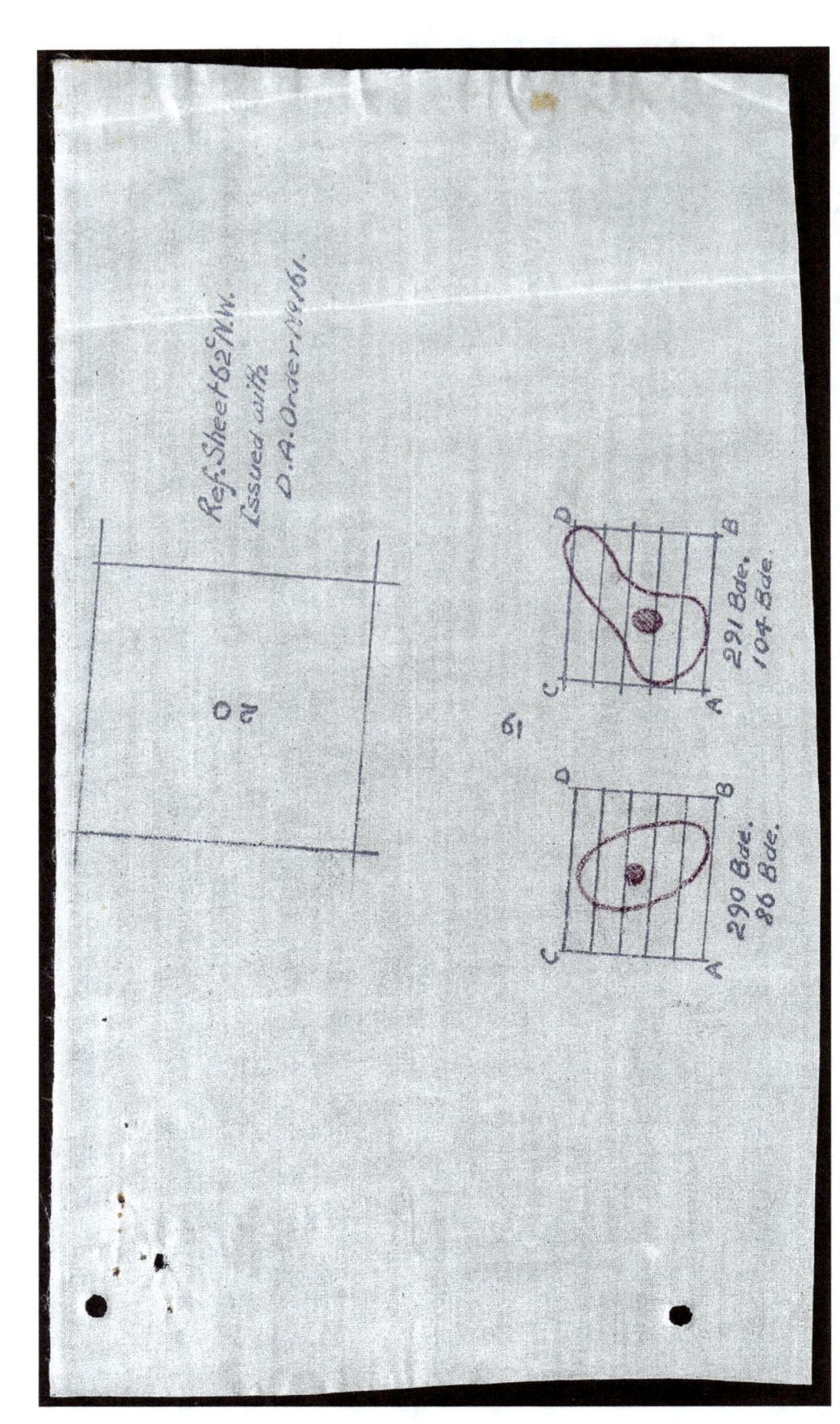

To all recipients of Operation

To all recipients of 58th D.A. Order No.161.

AMENDMENT No.1. to 58th D.A. Order No.161.

Co-ordinates for line "AB" for 291st and 104th Army Bdes. R.F.A. will be A.24.d.55.60 to A.24.d.55.00 and not as shewn on Tracing.
No fire South of the line "BD"

Para. 4 is cancelled.

Major,
Brigade Major, R.A.,
58th Divisional Artillery.

28th August 1918.

Copy No. 8

58th Divisional Artillery Order No. 162.

1. The advance will be continued tomorrow, 30th August, as rapidly as possible.

2. The advance guard has been detailed by the G.O.C. 58th Division as follows, under the command of the B.G.C. 175th Infantry Bde.
   175th Infantry Bde.   H.Q. at B.23.b.3.0.
   1/4th Suffolks.
   3 Brigades R.F.A.
   1 Section R.E.
   "C" and "D" Coys. M.G. Battalion.
   1 Company XXII Corps Cyclists.
   1 Squadron Northumberland Hussars.

3. The three Brigades R.F.A. will be the 86th, 291st and 290th. The latter will take over the Sector of the front bounded by East and West grid lines running through B.19.c.0.4. and B.19.a.0.8.
   The 104th Army Brigade R.F.A. will not advance with the Division but will rest in its present position, holding itself ready to advance at the shortest notice should the enemy resistance stiffen and additional Artillery be required. Meanwhile it will rest its personnel and horses to the utmost extent but keep in touch with 58th D.A.H.Q.

4. The advance will be continued by the mounted troops and cyclists who will be pushed forward at dawn, closely supported by the Artillery, on the lines already indicated in A.D.A. 430 dated 27th inst. and A.D.A. 432 dated 29th inst.

5. The number of guns required for the close support of the Infantry will be detailed by B.G.C. 175th Infantry Brigade and the officer in charge will immediately get into touch with the Battalions whom they are to support.

6. The B.G.C. 174th Infantry Brigade will take over from the B.G.C. 175th Infantry Brigade at 4.0 a.m. on the 31st inst., at which time the Artillery composing the advance guard will pass to his command.

7. A.1. Sub-Group (Major Sandford's) of Heavy Artillery will move forward as the situation develops and endeavour to keep under fire at the extremity of range any communications or bridges by which the enemy may be withdrawing his material.
   He will endeavour to keep in touch with B.G.C. Advanced Guard and answer calls made direct upon him for Heavy Artillery fire on any particular objectives.

8. Each Brigade of the Advanced Guard whose C.O. is unable to occupy Headquarters in sufficiently close proximity to those occupied by B.G.C. Advanced Guard will detail an experienced Liaison Officer to represent him there.

9. An A.R.P. is being established at A.23.b.53.

10. In moving forward, arrangements must be made via the Liaison Officers at Headquarters Advanced Guard to avoid congestion of traffic and Brigades will, if possible, only move one at a time.

11. Divisional /

2.

11. Divisional Artillery Headquarters will close at L.1.b.4.0. at 3 p.m. tomorrow, 30th inst., reopening at A.19.b.8.0.

12. ACKNOWLEDGE.

H. Williamson
Major,
Brigade Major R.A.,
58th Divisional Artillery.

29th August, 1918.

Copies to

86th Bde. R.F.A.	1
104th Bde. R.F.A.	2.
290th Bde. R.F.A.	3.
291st Bde. R.F.A.	4.
Sandford's Group	5.
71st Bde. R.G.A.	6.
27th Bde. R.G.A.	7.
58th Division "G"	8.
173rd Infy. Bde.	9.
174th Infy. Bde.	10.
175th Infy. Bde.	11.
3rd Aust. D.A.	12
25th D.A.	13
R.A., IIIrd Corps	14
H.A., IIIrd Corps	15

Prefix	Code		Words.	Charge.		No. of Message
Office of Origin and Service Instructions.			2		This message is on a/c of:	Recd. at ...... m.
			Sent			Date
			At ..... m.		..... Service.	From
			To			
			By		(Signature of "Franking Officer.")	By

TO
86
Tou 97 How 97 DH RA
290   58 Div. 174 +175th Bde

Sender's Number.	Day of Month.	In reply to Number.	
*KR.89	30		AAA

Reference Order 163 para 3 rate of barrage will be 100 yards in six minutes and not 100 yards in eight minutes as therein stated throughout area Acknowledge

From 58 D.A.
Place
Time 10.40 pm

* This line, except AAA, should be erased if not required.

SECRET.   Copy No. ...7....

58th Divisional Artillery Order No. 163.

1. The attack will be continued on MARRIERS WOOD tomorrow morning.

2. It will be covered by the following barrage of 18-pounders and 4.5" Hows. 100 yards East of it.

   At Zero   Opens on the line B.24.d.2.3. to B.18.b.2.0
                and remain till 0.20

   0.20   Creeps forward 100 yards every 8 minutes
                till it rests on the line C.19.d.0.3. -
                C.13.b.0.0 where it remains for 15 minutes.

                It then continues creeping forward 100 yards
                every 8 minutes till each gun rests on
                Protective Barrage from C.19.d.3.3. -
                C.20.a.0.0. - C.14.c.5.0. - C.14.a.6.0.

   Duration of fire on Protective Barrage will be 15 minutes.

   Rates of fire after leaving the WOOD will be governed by the ammunition supply.   Previous to this it will be normal.

3. Zones of fire will be allotted to 290th Bde. R.F.A. and 291st Bde. R.F.A. by O.C., 86th Army Bde. R.F.A.
   104th Army Bde. R.F.A. will superimpose its fire over the entire front covered by the barrage.

4. On conclusion of the Protective Barrage, no Artillery must be directed South of the following line :- C.25.a.0.0. - C.15.c.0.0. - C.17.c.0.0., as Australian troops will be operating in this area.

5. Zero hour will be 5.10 a.m., 31st August.

6. ACKNOWLEDGE.

                                                H. Williams
                                                       Major,
                                            Brigade Major, R.A.,
30th August 1918.   58th Divisional Artillery.

   Copies to
       86th Army Bde. R.F.A.   1
      104th Army Bde. R.F.A.   2
      290th Bde. R.F.A.   3
      291st Bde. R.F.A.   4
       71st Bde. R.G.A.   5
       27th Bde. R.G.A.   6
       58th Division "G"   7
      173rd Infy. Bde.   8
      174th Infy. Bde.   9
      175th Bde.   10
       3rd Aust. D.A.   11
       47th D.A.   12
       R.A., IIIrd Corps   13
       H.A., IIIrd Corps   14
       Staff Captain R.A.   15

S E C R E T. Copy No.

58th Divisional Artillery Order No.164.

1. 173rd Infantry Brigade will continue the attack tomorrow morning, September 1st.

2. The advance will be covered by a creeping barrage of 18 pounders which will act as follows :-

   O.O. Open on a line C.20.b.5.2. - C.20.b.0.4. - C.14.a.6.1. and remains till   0.15

   0.15 Lifts 100 yards and creeps at the rate of 100 yards every 5 minutes till it rests on the line of the Protective Barrage, C.16.d.8.7. - C.17.a.2.5. - C.11.c.0.9 - C.10.b.5.2., each gun remaining on the Protective Barrage Line and searching 300 yards beyond it until 2 hours 50 minutes after Zero, when fire will stop and further orders for its direction issued by B.G.C. 173rd Infy. Brigade.

   All lifts will be parallel to the portion of the Starting Line from C.20.b.0.4. - C.14.a.6.1.

3. 4.5" Hows. will conform, always keeping 100 yards E. of the 18-pounder barrage and concentrating their fire on likely spots in which the enemy might be collected.
   Corps H.A. are co-operating in the barrage within the limits of safety and also bombarding selected objectives.

4. Rates of fire.
   0.10 - 0.15   Rapid.
   0.15 - end.   Normal.

   Brigade Commanders will decrease the rate of fire to SLOW on their own Brigade front over localities which do not indicate the likely presence of hostile troops, but the NORMAL rate must be maintained through BOUCHAVESNES and over the Trench Systems in C.15. and 16. Care must be taken that ammunition is replenished early in case of hostile counter-attack.

5. Zones of fire will be allotted to 290th and 291st Brigades R.F.A. by O.C., 86th Army Brigade R.F.A. who will also allot targets to the Section of 144th Heavy Battery attached to him, as selected by B.G.C., 173rd Infy. Brigade.
   104th Army Brigade R.F.A. will fire the barrage over the following zone :-
   C.20.a.9.7. - C.11.c.2.0.
   C.14.c.7.8. - C.10.d.9.9.

6. The Boundary Line with the 3rd Australian Divisional Arty. on the South is - C.20.b.0.4. - C.20.b.5.2. - C.16.d.0.5. onwards.
   With the 47th Divisional Artillery on the North is - C.14.a.3.0. - C.10.central onwards.

7. Synchronisation will be done over the phone from D.A.H.Q.

8. Guns /

2.

8. Guns will be pushed forward in close support of the Infantry as on previous occasions, on the principle of 1 per battalion.

9. H.Q., 173rd Infantry Brigade will be on Hill 110 about B.23.central.

10. Zero hour will be 5.30 a.m.

11. ACKNOWLEDGE.

Major,
Brigade Major, R.A.,
58th Divisional Artillery.

31st August 1918.

Copies to

86th Army Bde. R.F.A.	1
104th Army Bde. R.F.A.	2
290th Brigade R.F.A.	3
291st Brigade R.F.A.	4
71st Brigade R.G.A.	5
27th Brigade R.G.A.	6
58th Division "G"	7
173rd Infantry Brigade	8
174th Infantry Brigade	9
175th Infantry Brigade.	10
3rd Aust. D.A.	11
47th D.A.	12
R.A., IIIrd Corps	13
H.A., IIIrd Corps.	14
Staff Captain R.A.	15
74th Divisional Arty.	16

86th Army Bde. R.F.A.
104th Army Bde. R.F.A.
290th Bde. R.F.A.
291st Bde. R.F.A.

A.D.A. 430

It is considered that valuable use can be made of air recuperator 18-pounders by harassing at extreme range the roads and tracks by which the enemy's rear formations are probably withdrawing material.

Each Artillery Brigade will detail one Section of 18-pounders with air recuperators to advance for the night to a previously reconnoitred position, as close as possible to our front line, from which they will fire at least 150 rounds per gun of H.E. with 106 fuze, on such objectives as -
(1) enemy's roads and tracks round MARRIERES WOOD
(2) Main road running North and South through C.14., 20., and 26, with sweeping fire.
(3) Road South of ROAD WOOD in C.26.

These targets are only allotted as an indication of the objectives which should be selected and it is left to the initiative of the Officers concerned to make the utmost use of the extreme range of their pieces, combined with the knowledge that the enemy is retiring and that his Artillery, especially for Counter-battery work is too disorganised to cause much inconvenience before the task has been completed and the guns withdrawn.

This will commence with 86th Army Bde. R.F.A. tomorrow night, 29th, followed on succeeding nights by 290th, 291st and 104 Brigades in the order given.

Major,
Brigade Major, R.A.,
58th Divisional Artillery.

28th August 1918.

Copy to 58th Division "G".

86th Army Bde. R.F.A.
104th Army Bde. R.F.A.
290th Bde. R.F.A.
291st Bde. R.F.A.

A.D.A. 432.

    Until definite touch is again obtained with an enemy line of resistance, 86th, 104th and 291st Brigade R.F.A. must rely definitely on the information they receive from H.Q., 175th Infantry Brigade, from whom they will receive their tactical instructions, and keep pushing forward their Brigades in echelons of batteries as close behind our infantry main line of advance as possible.

    290th Brigade R.F.A. will also endeavour to keep in touch with the situation locally but will still remain directly under the orders of these Headquarters.

    O.C., 290th Brigade R.F.A. will detail at least two guns from his Brigade, each under a subaltern, to push forward with the infantry occupying progressive positions of readiness from which they can quickly come into action at short range against the first definite obstacle which their officer can observe to be holding up the Infantry.

                                      Major,
                              Brigade Major, R.A.,
29th August 1918.   58th Divisional Artillery.

    Copy to 175th Infy. Bde.

SECRET.   BM/Y/ 441.

Sandford's Group.   58th Division "G"
86th Army Bde. R.F.A.   27th Brigade R.G.A.
173rd Infy. Bde.
174th Infy. Bde.
175th Infy. Bde.
_____

1. One Section of 60-pounders will be detailed from Sandford's Group to be directly under the orders of G.O.C., 58th Division.

   The Officer in charge will report to H.Q., 86th Army Bde. R.F.A. through whom he will receive orders.

2. The remainder of Sandford's Group reverts to command of O.C., 27th Bde. R.G.A. (H.Q. at present at L.1.a.8.2.)

3. The O.C. Detached Section will use his own initiative in pushing forward to support the Infantry and his rôle will be to engage as many targets as possible by direct observation, as well as to engage immediately any isolated enemy Artillery which is holding up the Infantry and whose position can be fairly accurately determined.

4. Report Centre of Advanced Guard today is at B.27.a.2.2.

5. ACKNOWLEDGE.

                                          H Williams
                                              Major,
                                       Brigade Major, R.A.,
30th August 1918.   58th Divisional Artillery.

58th DIVISIONAL ARTILLERY GROUP.

LOCATION STATEMENT.

Positions as at 6 p.m. 26th August, 1918.

58th D.A.H.Q. (Adv.) K.14.b.2.2.   (Rear) Billet No.44 HEILLY.

Unit.	Position.	
104th Army Bde.RFA, H.Q.	F.28.b.9.8.)	
"A" Battery.	F.29.a.4.2.)	
"B" Battery.	F.29.c.1.7.)	Covering Left Brigade.
"C" Battery.	F.29.a.2.5.)	
"D" Battery.	F.29.a.2.3.)	H.Q. 173rd Infantry Bde.
		F.21.d.3.0.
86th Army Bde.RFA, H.Q.	F.27.b.5.9.)	
"A" Battery.	L.10.b.)	
"B" Battery.	L.10.a.25.75.)	
"C" Battery.	F.29.a.2.2.)	
"D" Battery.	F.28.d.9.3.)	

250th Brigade R.F.A., H.Q.	F.28.d.2.4.)	
"A" Battery.	)	Covering Right Brigade.
"B" Battery.	)	
"C" Battery.	)	H.Q. 174th Infantry Bde.
"D" Battery.	)	
150th Army Bde.RFA. H.Q.	F.21.d.8.0.)	L.4.a.9.9.
"A" Battery.	F.21.d.9.4.)	
"B" Battery.	F.22.b.4.6.)	
"C" Battery.	F.22.c.1.8.)	
"D" Battery.	F.21.d.7.0.)	

291st Brigade R.F.A., H.Q.	L.4.a.6.7.)	
"A" Battery.	F.23.d.1.3.)	Superimposed over
"B" Battery.	F.28.b.7.5.)	
"C" Battery.	F.29.c.1.6.)	Divisional Front.
"D" Battery.	F.28.d.6.7.)	

Major Sandford's Group. H.Q. L.2.d.5.5.
120 Heavy Battery.4-60 pdrs. L.10.b.01.95.   Adv.W.L. K.18.c.60.50.
113 Heavy Battery.4-60 pdrs. L.3.c.85.45.   "   L.19.d.70.70.

58th D.A.C. SAILLY-LE-SEC.   58th D.T.M.O. No.1.Main St. HEILLY.

175th Infantry Brigade H.Q. L.1.b.3.0.

Forward Ammunition Refilling Point. E.18. central.

Lieut.
Reconnaissance Officer, R.A.
58th Divisional Artillery Group.

26th August.1918.

C O P Y.

58th DIVISIONAL ARTILLERY.

LOCATION STATEMENT.

Positions as at 6 p.m. 28th August 1918.

Advanced D.A.H.Q. L.1.b.30.20. Rear D.A.H.Q. K.14.b.20.20.

Unit.	Position.
290th Brigade R.F.A., H.Q.	F.28.b.60.72.
"A" Battery.	A.25.d.80.30.
"B" "	A.25.d.90.50.
"C" "	A.25.d.95.80.
"D" "	A.25.d.40.20.
291st Brigade R.F.A., H.Q.	F.30.c.30.00.
"A" Battery.	A.21.c.80.00.
"B" "	A.26.d.70.30.
"C" "	A.21.c.80.15.
"D" "	A.27.b.80.80.
86th Army Brigade R.F.A., H.Q.	F.27.b.30.80. — Moving to Copse "A"
"A" Battery.	A.20.d.50.80. A.20.c.90.90. on morning
"B" "	A.20.d.60.30. of 29th.
"C" "	A.20.d.50.90.
"D" "	A.20.d.40.50.
104th Army Brigade R.F.A., H.Q.	A.26.d.60.90.
"A" Battery.	A.27.b.65.30.
"B" "	A.27.b.65.40.
"C" "	A.27.d.70.70.
"D" "	A.27.b.65.95.
Major Sandford's Group. H.Q.	L.2.d.70.35.
113 Heavy Battery.	F.23.c.85.42.
120 Heavy Battery.	A.20.c.

Infantry Brigade H.Q. after re-arrangement tonight.
   173rd Infantry Brigade.   F.21.d.40.00.
   174th Infantry Brigade.   F.30.c.30.00.
   175th Infantry Brigade.   A.20.b.10.20.

58th D.A.C., H.Q.   K.24.a.60.30.
58th D.T.M.O.   No.1 Main Street, REILLY.

A.R.P.s
   Forward.   L.15.b.20.70.
                K.17.central.
                K.13.d.4.2.

(sgd) N.F.Palmer, Lieut.
Reconnaissance Officer, R.A.
28th August 1918.   58th Divisional Artillery.

58th DIVISIONAL ARTILLERY.

LOCATION STATEMENT.   Ref. Sheets. 62.d. & 62.c.

Positions as at 9 a.m. 1st September, 1918.

Advanced D.A.H.Q.   A.19.b.8.0.   Rear D.A.H.Q.   L.1.b.3.2.

Unit.	Position.
290th Brigade R.F.A., H.Q.	B.27.b.40.00.
"A" Battery.	B.24.c.00.25.
"B" "	~~B.23.d.95.25.~~ B.23.d.95.95.
"C" "	B.22.d.50.50.
"D" "	B.30.a.70.45.
291st Brigade R.F.A., H.Q.	B.23.a.70.20.
"A" Battery.	B.24.a.
"B" "	B.23.a.
"C" "	B.24.a.
"D" "	B.30.a.
86th Army Brigade R.F.A., H.Q.	B.23.c.60.80.
"A" Battery.	B.23.b.10.60.
"B" "	B.22.d.20.40.
"C" "	B.24.a.20.20.
"D" "	B.23.a.60.20.
104th Army Brigade R.F.A., HQ.	B.29.b.00.80.
"A" Battery.	B.30.c.20.20.
"B" "	B.30.c.20.20.
"C" "	B.30.c.20.30.
"D" "	B.30.c.80.50.

58th D.A.C.	A.28.b.70.50.
A.R.P.(advanced)	A.23.b.50.30.
58th D.T.M.O.	No.1, Main Street, HEILLY.
173rd Infantry Brigade H.Q.	Hill 110, B.23.d.
174th Infantry Brigade H.Q.	B.27.a.0.0.
175th Infantry Brigade H.Q.	Quarry, A.28.a.

Attached.
Section 114 H.B.	(60-pdrs)	B.15.c.30.50. (approx)

   (sgd) N.F.Palmer, Lieut.
   Reconnaissance Officer, R.A.
   58th Divisional Artillery.

31st August 1918.

Vol. 21.

War Diary

58th D.A.

Sept. 1918

Army Form C.2118.

WAR-DIARY
or
INTELLIGENCE-SUMMARY.
H.Q., 58th Divisional Artillery.

September, 1918.

Vol 21

(Erase heading not required.)

Instructions regarding War Diaries and Intelligence Summaries are contained in F.S. Regs., Part II. and the Staff Manual respectively. Title pages will be prepared in manuscript.

Place	Date	Hour	Summary of Events and Information	Remarks and references to Appendices
A.19.b.8.0. CARNOY.	1st	-	The attack was continued by the 173rd Infantry Brigade, the barrage opening on a line C.20.b.5.2., C.20.b.0.4. - C.14.a.6.1. with a protective barrage on C.16.d.8.7. - C.17.a.2.5. - C.11.c.0.9., C.10.b.5.2. batteries pushing forward in close support of the Infantry.	
RAILHEAD.	2nd.	4 p.m.	The C.R.A. 58th Division handed over the Artillery covering the 58th Divisional front consisting of 290, 291, Brigades R.F.A. and 86th and 104th Army Brigades R.F.A. and one section of 60-pounders at B.15.c.30.50, to C.R.A., 74th Division. The orders for the barrage, which included some smoke, to cover the attack of the 229th Infantry Brigade, 74th Division, with objectives D.10.c.0.0. - D.10.a.2.0 - D.4.c.0.0. - D.3.b.0.0. D.2.b.0.0. were issued, by C.R.A. 58th Division, and the brigades were moved up in order to secure the maximum range possible. Locations of Brigade H.Q. which were in close proximity to their batteries were as follows:- 290th Brigade R.F.A. B.30.b.6.4. ; 291st Brigade R.F.A. B.30.b.9.8. : 86th Army Brigade R.F.A. B.23.c.2.5. : 104th Army Brigade R.F.A. B.29.d.0.8. Two guns of each of the above brigades moved forward with the infantry and by close co-operation with the latter did very effective work on enemy personnel in the open. The command of the R.F.A. Brigades passed to B.G.C. 229th Infantry Brigade from zero onwards.	

Army Form C. 2118.

WAR DIARY
or
INTELLIGENCE SUMMARY.
(Erase heading not required.)

Instructions regarding War Diaries and Intelligence Summaries are contained in F.S. Regs., Part II. and the Staff Manual respectively. Title pages will be prepared in manuscript.

- 2 -

Place	Date	Hour	Summary of Events and Information	Remarks and references to Appendices
A.19.b.8.0.	3 - 6th.		Rested at CARNOY RAILHEAD. Brigades still being in line under C.R.A., 74th Division.	
CARNOY	7th.		Moved forward to G.20.central, a quarry in Eastern side of COMBLES - PERONNE Road and South of BOUCHAVESNES. Took over from the 47th Division, the brigades in line being 290th Brigade (H.Q.D.17.d.2.4.) 291st Brigade R.F.A. (H.Q.D.23.b.0.7.) 110th and 112th Brigades R.F.A. (H.Q.E.13.c.7.7.) Division on Left, 12th. Division on Right, 74th.	
D.22.a.4.1.	8th		Moved again to Western edge of GURLU WOOD (D.22.a.4.1.) Divisional front from dawn today being bounded on the South by the East and West Grid through F.7.c.0.0. and on the North by East and West Grid through X.19.c.0.0. 290th, 62nd and 108th (Army) Brigades R.F.A. being in the line, and 291st Brigade R.F.A. resting as D.23.b.0.7. O.C., 290th Bde.RFA in close liaison with the 175th Infantry Brigade with combined H.Q. at W.25.c.4.5. 113th Heavy Battery, R.G.A. (60-pounders) at E.26.b.80.65 also attached. Artillery also available, but in Corps Reserve, in TORTILLE VALLEY, 63rd, 82nd and 83rd Brigades R.F.A., the last named being in CATAPILLAR VALLEY.	
"	9th.		47th Brigade R.G.A. with H.Q. at D.26.b.0.8. are affiliated to the 58th D.A. Batteries were given a fixed amount of ammunition per day from this date.	
"	9th.		Locations 290th Bde.RFA (H.Q.W.25.c.4.5. batteries in E.9.c, E.14.c, E.15.a. & c.	

WAR DIARY or INTELLIGENCE SUMMARY.

Army Form C. 2118.

(Erase heading not required.)

Place	Date	Hour	Summary of Events and Information	Remarks and references to Appendices
D.22.a.4.1.	9th.		B91st Brigade R.F.A. (H.Q., D.23.a.9.7., with batteries in D.22.b., D.18.a. and D.23.b. 62nd Brigade R.F.A. (H.Q. E.7.b.5.3. with batteries in E.8.d. and C/62 with battalion at E.4.c. central where this battery did very effective work against personnel in the open, engaging parties of 40 and 70 of the enemy and inflicting heavy casualties. A quiet day.	
	10th.		The 173rd Infantry Brigade attacked EPEHY and PEZIERES at 5.15 a.m, the artillery barrage being divided as follows :- 108th and 62nd Bdes.RFA opened on a line W.30.a.3.4. to E.6.a.65.80. and 290 and 291st Bdes.RFA E.6.d.55.35 to F.7.a.1.7. all batteries putting down a final protective barrage along the line F.1.b.5.1. - F.1.a.95.70 - X.25.c.5.6. - X.25.a.15.40. and W.30.b.8.9. Our Trench Mortars bombarded selected strong points on road running S.E. through EPEHY and PEZIERES from Zero to Zero plus 30 minutes. The gap between the two barrages being covered by a Machine Gun barrage. 4.5" Hows fired on the following selected points F.8.c.10.55. F8.a.3.1. - F.8.a.35.75 - F.2.c.1.6. - F.1.b.6.5. and X.25.a.05.85. The infantry reached objective about 8.45 a.m. but had to retire due to insufficient support and took up a line approx. as follows - Sunken roads in E.12.b. & d. - E.6.d.8.0 - E.6.b.6.0. E.6.b.3.8 - TOTTENHAM POST but had to retire again before nightfall due to heavy M.G. and some shelling, to a general line of trenches in W.29.b.&d - E.5.b.& d.	

Army Form C. 2118.

WAR DIARY
or
INTELLIGENCE SUMMARY.
(Erase heading not required.)

Instructions regarding War Diaries and Intelligence Summaries are contained in F. S. Regs., Part II. and the Staff Manual respectively. Title pages will be prepared in manuscript.

- 4 -

Place	Date	Hour	Summary of Events and Information	Remarks and references to Appendices
D.22.a.4.1.	10th.		with 150 men in road through E.12.central and along road from F.7.c.0.8. to E.12.d.8.0. with 2 Companys on a N & S line through E.11.central, thence Capron Copse trench as far as Railway in E.18.b. where they were in touch with 74th Div. (Div.on our Right) Posts were established at TOTTENHAM POST and W.30.a.0.5.	
	11th.		Our Infantry worked forward without artillery preparations and occupied trenches in E.12.a. & b. with posts at E.12.a.0.9 - E.12.a.4.8., covering the gap between these and our line in E.5.b. and d.	
	12th.		At 9 a.m. after a hurricane bombardment by T.Ms and smothering the Garrisons with stick bombs the enemy rushed TOTTENHAM POST and occupied same.	
	13th.		A hostile flammenwerfer attack by 21st Div. ◊ on our Left) completely repulsed - some prisoners taken without any casualties being incurred.	
	14th.		Artillery and T.Ms co-operated with fire during gas projection on PEZIERES and EPEHY at 2 a.m. An extremely quiet day no change in general situation. Another T.M. was placed in position at W.29.d.25.15.	

WAR DIARY
or
INTELLIGENCE SUMMARY.
(Erase heading not required.)

Army Form C. 2118.

Place	Date	Hour	Summary of Events and Information	Remarks and references to Appendices
D.22.a.4.1.	15/17.		No material changes in the line, Batteries and Headquarters remaining in the same positions till 6 p.m. on the 17th, when the following re-adjustment of artillery took place. 290, 291, and 62nd Brigades R.F.A. passed to 18th D.A., on the right of our Divisional front. The 108th Army Brigade R.F.A.(with H.Q. and batteries at E.1.c.2.2. and E.3.a. and c) and the 63rd Brigade R.F.A.(with H.Q. and batteries at E.3.c.0.8. and W.28.b, E.3.d, E.4.a.& c) formed the artillery to cover the attack of 173rd Infantry Brigade on PEIZERE and German Trench system E. of the village. The 21st Division of V Corps were on the left, and the 12th Division on the right. Zero hour was 5.20 a.m. and the barrage opened on the following start line E.6.a.5.3. to W.24.c.5.0., the 63rd Brigade R.F.A. being on the right and the 108th Army Brigade R.F.A. on the left positions. The objective for the 58th Division was limited to POPLAR TRENCH from X.26.a.9.9. to its junction with ROOM TRENCH and FIR SUPPORT in X.26.c. after which the 12th and 21st Divisions were to meet and advance to their second objective. Heavies and our T.M.s co-operated in the attack by bombarding suitable strong points behind the enemy lines. Our T.Ms were sited in a trench at W.29.d.2.2. By 10 a.m. MC.PHEE POST, MC.LEAN and MORGAN POSTS were reported captured and by 10.45 a.m. the 2/2nd Londons reported the capture of FIR SUPPORT and POPLAR TRENCH	

- 5 -

WAR DIARY
or
INTELLIGENCE SUMMARY.
(Erase heading not required.)

Army Form C. 2118.

- 6 -

Place	Date	Hour	Summary of Events and Information	Remarks and references to Appendices
			with 2 coys. of 2/24th Londons in Railway at X.25. Here considerable opposition was encountered and parties of the enemy made their reappearance in PEIZERE and retarded the advance of the 12th Division in EPEHY. At 12.30 p.m. a strong counter-attack from LINNET VALLEY was repulsed and prisoners taken. The 63rd Brigade R.F.A. and 108th Army Brigade RFA formed a defensive flank barrage on the following lines X.27.c.5.0 - X.28.b.0.0. - X.28.b.6.5. - X.22.d.7.0.	
		1 pm.	Reports indicated that 21st Division had done well and were east of BEET FACTORY in X.14.a. and held positions of BEET and VILLERS GUISLAIN Trenches. (FISHER'S KEEP)	
		2.5 pm.	12th Division report EPEHY now practically clear of enemy but one strong point (FISHER'S KEEP) was not finally cleared up till 7.35 p.m. when 3rd Battalion reported this point mopped up.	
		2.45 pm.	The general situation was as follows, the 58th Div. held POPLAR TRENCH and FIR SUPPORT and CHESTNUT AVENUE but were not in touch with the 12th on their right, but at 3.50 p.m. the 173rd Infantry Brigade reported that a hostile counter-attack from the S.E. had captured POPLAR TRENCH and we were holding FIR SUPPORT. Steps were at once taken to recapture POPLAR TRENCH with help from 63rd and 108th (Army) Brigades R.F.A. At 6 p.m. the	

WAR DIARY
or
INTELLIGENCE SUMMARY.
(Erase heading not required.)

Army Form C. 2118.

- 7 -

Place	Date	Hour	Summary of Events and Information	Remarks and references to Appendices
			Infantry reported that we held a line as follows, FIR SUPPORT from X.26.a.4.2. westwards to Northern Divisional Boundary, we also hold line of Railway and PRINCE RESERVE in K.25. It is definitely established that German still hold CHESTNUT AVENUE and positions of LARK SPUR in F.1.b. - X.25.d. and CULLEN POST. At 6.30 p.m. the 108th Army Brigade R.F.A. was placed under the direct orders of B.G.C., 173rd Infantry. The S.O.S. Lines for the 108th Army Brigade R.F.A. joined those of the 21st Division at X.21.c.0.0. and were arranged Southwards from here by direct consultation with B.G.C., 173rd Infantry. At 11.15 p.m. orders were issued for the 173rd Infantry Brigade to establish themselves in POPLAR TRENCH in X.26.b. with post down ROOM TRENCH and touch obtained with 12th Division in CHESTNUT AVENUE. Heavy harassing fire was maintained all night and during early morning on CATELET VALLEY and KILDARE AVENUE X.27.	
	19th.		At 2.30 a.m. the Infantry reported the occupation of Northern end of POPLAR TRENCH to X.26.a.9.9. and were working southwards. No touch with 12th Division on their right as Germans reported still holding CHESTNUT AVENUE. At 7 a.m. the general situation was as follows we held POPLAR TRENCH from X.26.a.9.9. to X.26.b.2.6., 12th Division have captured CHESTNUT AVENUE and established a post at X.26.a.5.0.	

Army Form C. 2118.

WAR DIARY
or
INTELLIGENCE SUMMARY.
(Erase heading not required.)

Instructions regarding War Diaries and Intelligence Summaries are contained in F.S. Regs., Part II. and the Staff Manual respectively. Title pages will be prepared in manuscript.

Place	Date	Hour	Summary of Events and Information	Remarks and references to Appendices
			- 8 -	
	19th.	11 - 11.20 a.m.	173rd Brigade bombarded POPLAR TRENCH from X.26.b.3.7. to junction of POPLAR and ROOM TRENCHES with trench mortars., The 12th Division again attacking under a barrage on the following lines F.9.c.7.9. to X.26.c.4.1. at the same time. 108th Army Brigade R.F.A. kept close touch with 173rd Brigade throughout these operations from their new H.Q. at W.28.a.9.3. with their 18-pounder batteries in W.29.b. and 4.5" Howitzer batteries at E.5.c.central which positions were occupied at 3 p.m. on the 18th. Reports at 8.30 p.m. shew that we hold the whole of POPLAR TRENCH and are pushing down ROOM TRENCH with no opposition from the enemy. T.M. dispositions at 7 a.m. on 19th as follows, H.Q. LIERAMONT, 2. 6" Newton Mortars at W.29.d.2.2., 1 at E.12.a.4.4., 1 at E.12.a.60.35 and 2 German minenwerfers at E.12.a.4.4. - E.12.a.5.4.	
	20/21st & 21/22nd.		No further attacks undertaken on these days and artillery dispositions remained the same. At 9.30 p.m. the 175th Infantry Brigade attacked, the objectives being KILDARE POST and LANE and road running south to X.28.cent, also SPRINT ROAD and DADOS LOOP. The Infantry formed up on a line running North and South through X.27.a.5.9. The attack was covered by the 108th Army Brigade R.F.A. who harassed approaches to and bombarded the objectives during the afternoon. A standing barrage was formed on the objectives at 9.30 p.m. on the	

T1134. Wt. W708—776. 500000. 4/15. Sir J. C. & S.

WAR DIARY or INTELLIGENCE SUMMARY.

Army Form C. 2118.

- 9 -

Place	Date	Hour	Summary of Events and Information	Remarks and references to Appendices
	23rd		line X.28.b.1.4. to X.22.c.5.0. from which line the barrage lifted at 10.5 p.m. and further orders were issued by B.G.C., 175th Infantry Brigade. The 33rd Division on the left attacked LIMERICK POST and the 12th Division on the right of our Divisional Front. Heavies co-operated by bombarding BIRD CAGE in X.29.d., KILDARE POST, SPRINT ROAD and OSSUS WOOD during the afternoon. The attack was a success, objectives being taken by 9th Londons and 4th Suffolks by midnight. An attempt to establish an international post at X.22.c.5.5. with the 33rd Division failed. Minor counter-attacks by the enemy on our right failed and heavy casualties were inflicted by our barrage. The 44th Brigade, 74th D.A., relieved the 108th Army Brigade R.F.A. in their positions as follows:- H.Q., W.28.a.9.3. A/108, W.29.b.5.2., B/108 W.29.b.7.0., C/108 W.29.b.5.5., and D/108 E.5.d.9.8., during the morning, starting at 10.30 a.m., The 108th Army Brigade RFA proceeding to the Wagon Lines vacated by the 44th Brigade R.F.A. in E.28.b. and d. and then proceeded into action under 74th D.A. on the night of 23/24th September. The 58th Division were relieved in the line by the 12th Division on the night of 23/24 and command of the Artillery passed to G.O.C., R.A 12th Division. On completion of this relief, which was about midnight, O.C., 44th Brigade R.F.A. kept in close liaison with O.C., 63rd Brigade RFA,	

Army Form C. 2118.

WAR DIARY
or
INTELLIGENCE SUMMARY.
(Erase heading not required.)

Instructions regarding War Diaries and Intelligence Summaries are contained in F.S. Regs., Part II. and the Staff Manual respectively. Title pages will be prepared in manuscript.

- 10 -

Place	Date	Hour	Summary of Events and Information	Remarks and references to Appendices
	24th.		(H.Q. at E.4.c.6.5.) under whom he was grouped, then the 12th Division took over. The T.M.s in PEZIERE withdrew to LIERAMONT before night. Enemy counter-attacks throughout day failed to penetrate our line in any Sector and much execution was done by our Artillery which took full advantage of the enemy formations in the open. The line on relief ran as follows :- CATELET COPSE, SPRINT ROAD, DADOS LOOP, DADOS LANE, and KILLARE LANE, continued on North by 33rd Division, V Corps, along LIMERICK POST and trench and MEATH POST, the 12th Division on the right, holding BRAYTON POST, HEYTHORP POST and LITTLE PRIEL FARM to CATELET COPSE.	
	25th.		H.Q.R.A., 58th Division remained in GURLU WOOD, the units of the D.A. came under C.R.A., 4th Australian Division, covering the front held by 27th American Division.	
	26th.		290th and 291st Brigades supported the attacks of the 27th American Division to gain a footing for the general attack on the HINDENBURG LINE.	
	29th.		HINDENBURG LINE and GOUY and LE CATELET captured.	
	30th.		290th and 291st Brigades came under C.R.A., 3rd Australian Division at 1.30 a.m.	

Maxwell
Brigadier General,
C.R.A., 58th Division.

Brigade Major,
    III Corps, H.A.

        58th Divisional Artillery require the following shelling :-

        Harassing fire on EPEHY and PEIZIERE especially approaches thereto during the night, also on CEMETERY in F.1.b. and Machine Guns in RAILWAY CUTTING EMBANKMENT in F.1.a. and F.1.b. (this is in 12th Division area and their consent will be required.)

        Crashes during the night on :-
        OLD COPSE.   F.9.a.
        TETARD WOOD.   F.2.a.
        Sunken Light Railway. F.2.c.
        ENFER WOOD.   F.9.d.
        No.12 Copse.   F.3.b.
        KNOLL POST.   F.8.d.
        DEELISH POST.   F.8.d.

        Bombardment commencing at Zero hour (presumably 7.30 a.m.) 8th inst.

    Zero to Zero plus 30 mins.   -   60 pdrs. to fire Shrapnel on
                                      Railway Embankment in F.1.b. & d.,
                                      F.2.c. and F.7.b. and c.

    Zero to Zero plus 90 mins.   -   Bombard selected points in old
                                      British trench X.28., F.5 - F.11.
                                      and F.12. (If possible, with aerial
                                      observation.) -

                                      GRAFTON POST.   (F.5.c.)
                                      KILDARE POST.   (X.28.b.)
                                      LITTLE PRIEL FARM. (X.28.d.)
                                      HEYTHORP POST.   (F.4.b.)
                                      FLEECEALL POST.   (F.11.b.)
                                      LIMERICK POST.   (X.21.d.)
                                      ISLAND TRAVERSE. (F.12.c.)

        Counter Battery on likely areas in which N.Fs. were received this afternoon.

        I am obliged to send this information through to you in the hope that you will detail either 47 Brigade or any other Brigade you deem fit to carry out these tasks as I am out of communication with 47 Brigade R.G.A.

                                                Lieut, R.G.A.
7/9/18.   Liaison Officer, 58th Divisional Arty.

    Copies to :-
        58th Division. "G"
        290th Brigade R.F.A.
        174th Infantry Brigade.

SECRET.  Copy No. ......7....

58th Divisional Artillery Order No. 165.

1. The 229th Infantry Brigade, 74th Division, is continuing the attack tomorrow morning September 2nd, to capture the objectives
   D.10.c.0.0. - D.10.a.2.0. - D.4.c.0.0. - D.3.b.0.0. - D.2.b.0.0.

2. The Divisional Boundaries are as detailed in R.N. 102 dated 1st September (sent to those concerned only)

3. The Artillery Brigades to cover the attack will be approximately as follows by 12 midnight, September 1st/2nd.

86th Army Bde. R.F.A.	C.13.c.
290th Brigade R.F.A.	C.19.a. and b.
291st Brigade R.F.A.	C.19.c. and d.
104th Army Brigade R.F.A.	B.30.c.

   At least 400 rounds per gun will be required in each position and 104th Army Brigade R.F.A. will ~~also have 50 rounds per gun of smoke shell.~~ arrange for 6 18-pdrs to have 140 rds of smoke shell and 200 rds of ordinary and the remainder 300 rds of ordinary.

4. The 18-pounder Creeping Barrage covering the attack will act as follows :-

   0.0   Open on line C.29.b.4.2 - C.16.b.4.0 - C.11.c.1.1.
                and remain till   0.15

   0.15 Creep forward 100 yards in 5 minutes till it reaches the line D.15.a.2.5. - D.2.c.6.8. (i.e. a depth of 4000 yards.)

   To reach this line, every gun must fire to the extremity of its range.
   The Barrage fire after reaching this line is being taken up by two Brigades of the 74th Divisional Artillery, who are moving forward as soon as the Infantry are well on the way, under orders which are being issued separately.
   → all lifts will be parallel to the position of the start line between C.29.b.042 and C.16.b.4.0.

5. The 4.5" Howitzers will conform to the 18-pounder barrage keeping 100 yards East of it and concentrating on definite features which are likely to harbour enemy troops or M.G. nests.

6. The O.C. Section of 144th Heavy Battery will have targets detailed to him by B.G.C. 229th Infantry Brigade, which will be transmitted by O.C. 290th Brigade R.F.A., with whom he will get into touch at ~~B.30.b.5.5.~~ C.25.b.5.2.

7. IIIrd Corps Heavy Artillery are co-operating throughout as shewn in Appendix "A".

8. Headquarters 229th Infantry Brigade is being established at ~~B.30.b.5.5.~~, where Lt. Col. W.A.F. Jones, D.S.O., Commdg. C.25.b.5.2 290th Brigade R.F.A. will also be and all Brigade Commanders will keep in close touch with him.
   Two guns per Brigade, each under an Officer, will be detailed to push forward in close support of the Infantry. They will act entirely independently and the officers will keep in direct touch with the advancing Infantry.

9. Boundaries /

SEEN BY:-
G.O.C.......
G.S.O.I......
G.S.O.II......
G.S.O.III......

2.

9. Boundaries between zones will be as follows :-

   291st Brigade R.F.A.   C.29.b.4.2. - D.15.a.2.5.
                       and C.23.c.8.4. - D.8.d.7.6.

   290th Brigade R.F.A.   C.23.c.8.4. - D.8.d.7.6.
                       and C.16.d.9.1. - D.8.b.0.9.

   86th Army Bde. R.F.A.   C.16.d.9.1. - D.8.b.0.9.
                       and C.11.c.1.1. - D.2.c.6.8.

10. 104th Army Brigade R.F.A. will perform the following special tasks :-
    1 18-pdr. battery superimposed over zone of 86th Army Brigade R.F.A.
    1 4.5" How. battery superimposed on zone of 290th Brigade R.F.A.
    1 18-pdr. battery fires a smoke barrage to blind the South end of MOISLAINS, C.17.d.8.4. - C.18.c.8.2.

    Smoke Barrage will commence at Zero and lift at Zero plus 75 minutes and join the 18-pounder Creeping Barrage of 290th Brigade R.F.A.
    Care must be taken to put down the smoke barrage well to windward of the area to be blinded.

    The guns of 104th Army Brigade R.F.A. will become out of range early in the action and will have the teams ready for an immediate advance, if ordered to, in which case they should be prepared to advance to positions from which they can bring fire to bear upon NURLU.

11. 86th, 290th and 291st Brigades R.F.A. will be prepared to advance immediately the Final Objectives have been definitely made good and will do so in the following order :-
    86th Army Brigade R.F.A.
    290th Brigade R.F.A.
    291st Brigade R.F.A.
    keeping in that order from North to South and occupying positions from which they can cover the North and South Grid line through D.5. cent.
    They will receive the order to advance as the situation permits from B.G.C. 229th Infantry Brigade from whom they will receive all further instructions from Zero onwards.

12. Rates of fire.
          0.0 - 0.15   SLOW
          0.15 onwards   NORMAL.

    Brigade Commanders will arrange to quicken the rate of fire to RAPID for individual guns as they pass over important objectives, and 104th Army Brigade R.F.A. will fire at NORMAL rate throughout.

13. Watches will be synchronised by phone from H.Q. 74th Divl. Artillery at H.3.b.4.6.

14. Zero Hour will be 5.30 a.m., September 2nd.

15. ACKNOWLEDGE.

H Williams
Major,
Brigade Major, R.A.,
58th Divisional Artillery.

1st September 1918.

Distribution.

86th Army Brigade R.F.A.	1
104th Army Bde. R.F.A.	2
290th Bde. R.F.A.	3
291st Bde. R.F.A.	4
71st Brigade R.G.A.	5
27th Brigade R.G.A.	6
58th Division "G"	7
74th Division "G"	8
173rd Infy. Bde.	9
229th Infy. Brigade	10 11 12
74th Divisional Arty.	13 14 15
3rd Aust. D.A.	16
47th D.A.	17
R.A., IIIrd Corps	18
H.A., IIIrd Corps	19
Staff Captain, R.A.	20

Appendix "A".

Heavy Artillery.

Heavy Artillery will co-operate as follows :-

1. Zero - Zero plus 1 hour 15 minutes.

    Bombard MOISLAINS, lifting off portion in C.18.c. and C.17.d. at Zero plus 45 minutes.

2. Zero plus 1 hour 15 mins - Zero plus 1 hour 30 mins.

    Search MONASTIR TRENCH in D.7.d. and D.8.c. and Trenches D.13.d. to D.14.a.6.0.

3. Zero plus 1 hour 30 mins - Zero plus 2 hours 35 mins.

    Search Trench system from D.8.b.1.0. to D.14.c.9.2.

4. Zero plus 2 hours 35 mins - Zero plus 3 hours.

    Search Woods and Quarries in D.9.d. and D.15.a.

5. Zero plus 3 hours - Zero plus 4 hours.

    Bombard NURLU and Trench Systems in D.10.a., D.10.d., D.9.d.

6. Zero plus 4 hours - Zero plus 4 hours 30 mins.

    Harass roads and Tracks in D.5 and LIERMONT TRENCH D.11., D.12., West of safety limits from N. and S. Grid Line through D.5.c.0.0. Heavy Artillery will put down a Protective Barrage on these areas, if called upon after Zero plus 4 hours 30 mins.

AMENDMENTS NO. 1 to 58th D.A. Order No. 165.

Para. 3.   Delete last two lines and substitute :-

"and 104th Army Bd . R.F.A. will arrange for 6 18-pdrs. to have 140 rounds of Smoke Shell and 200 rounds of ordinary and the remainder 300 rounds of ordinary."

Para. 4.   Add.

"All lifts will be parallel to the portion of the START LINE between C.20.b.4.2. and C.16.b.4.0."

Para. 6.   Last line.

For "B.30.b.5.5." read "C.25.b.5.2."

Para. 8.   2nd Line.

For "B. 30 .b.5.5." read "C.25.b.5.2."

ACKNOWLEDGE.
done

                                                H. Williamson
                                                    Major,
                                            Brigade Major, R.A.,
1st September 1918.   58th Divisional Artillery.

OO165 amended

SEEN BY:-
G.O.C.........
G.S.O.I........
G.S.O.II.......
G.S.O.III......
....

SECRET.   Copy No. ....

58th Divisional Artillery Order No. 166.

1. At dawn tomorrow, 8th September, the front covered by the 58th Division will be bounded on the South by the East and West grid through F.7.c.0.0 and on the North by the East and West grid through L.19.c.0.0.

2. The Artillery available will be 290th, 291st, 108th and 62nd Brigades R.F.A., of which 291st Brigade R.F.A. will be resting but will be liable to be called upon at any moment.

3. Lt. Col. W.A.F. JONES, commanding 290th Brigade R.F.A. will get into immediate touch with B.G.C. 174th Infantry Brigade at W.25.c.2.5. and will transmit his orders to the remaining Brigades as required, who must keep in touch with him throughout.

4. O.C., 113 Heavy Battery will also receive orders direct through O.C., 290th Brigade R.F.A.

5. ACKNOWLEDGE.

                                                    Major,
                                            Brigade Major, R.A.,
6th September 1918.   58th Divisional Artillery.

    Copies to
        290th Brigade R.F.A.   1
        291st Brigade R.F.A.   2
        108th Army Brigade R.F.A.   3
         62nd Brigade R.F.A.   4
        110th Brigade R.F.A.   5
        112th Brigade R.F.A.   6
        113rd Heavy Battery.   7
        58th Division.   8
        173rd Infy. Bde.   9
        174th Infy. Bde.   10
        175th Infy. Bde.   11
        74th D.A.   12
        21st D.A.   13
        R.A., IIIrd Corps   14
        H.A., IIIrd Corps   15
        Staff Captain, R.A.   16
        Liaison Officer.   17
        Signals Officer R.A.   18
        R.O.R.A.   19
        12th D.A.   20

SECRET.   Copy No...... - 8 SEP. 1918

58th Divisional Artillery Order No. 167.

1.   The situation with regard to the Artillery at present allotted to the 58th Division is as follows :-

   (a)   Covering the front line from S. to N. in the order named -

   (1) In action.
           290th Brigade R.F.A.
           62nd Brigade R.F.A.
           108th Army Brigade R.F.A.
           113th Heavy Battery R.G.A.(over whole front)

   (2) In rest, but ready to operate at short notice without reference to higher authority -
           291st Brigade R.F.A.

   (b)   In reserve, occupying wagon lines in the TORTILLE Valley, and only available with the sanction of G.O.C., IIIrd Corps R.A. -
           63rd Brigade R.F.A.
           82nd Brigade R.F.A.
           83rd Brigade R.F.A.   (CATERPILLAR VALLEY.)

   If the advance continues these brigades will be moved forward under orders from C.R.A., 58th Division to new wagon lines from which they can come into action at short notice, if required.

   (c)   Heavy Artillery, in addition to 113th Heavy Battery, RGA, has been detailed by the B.G.C., III Corps H.A. as follows -
           47th Brigade R.G.A. affiliated to the 58th Division.
           23rd Brigade R.G.A. reinforcing the 47th Brigade RGA.

2.   All ammunition left in vacated positions by the brigades detailed in para. 1 (b) will be collected under their own arrangements and deposited at the 58th A.R.P. at D.11.d.9.7.
   A notification will be sent to this office of the amount so dumped. In addition, the 18th D.A.C. will clear the A.R.P. at RANCOURT and transfer the ammunition to the same place, reporting completion and the amount of ammunition so shifted.

3.   Communication with units as far as orderlies are concerned will be maintained as follows :-

   (a) At Headquarters, 290th Brigade R.F.A. W.25.c.2.5. orderlies from -
           62nd Brigade R.F.A.
           108th Army Brigade R.F.A.
           113th Heavy Battery, R.G.A.
   Orders for above units will be sent to H.Q. 290th Brigade R.F.A. for distribution, by D.R. from Headquarters, 58th Divisional Artillery.

   (b) At Headquarters, 58th Divisional Artillery, D.21.b.9.9. orderlies from -
           290th Brigade R.F.A.
           291st Brigade R.F.A.
           63rd Brigade R.F.A.
           82nd Brigade R.F.A.
           83rd Brigade R.F.A.
           113th Heavy Battery, R.G.A.
           47th Brigade R.G.A.
           58th D.A.C.

   (c)   It is impressed on all units the utmost importance of sending a fresh orderly, on completion of a move of Headquarters to relieve the one who only knows the location of the old ones.

(2)

4. A fixed ammunition allotment has now been made to the Division, and in accordance with the situation, a proportion of it will be allowed to Brigades for *daily* expenditure. This will be notified by wire.
   In case of a hostile attack, however, ammunition will be used as required.

5. All arrangements for liaison will be made direct, as before, with O.C., 290th Brigade R.F.A. by B.G.C., Infantry Brigade holding the line.

6. ACKNOWLEDGE.

H. Williamson
Major,
Brigade Major, R.A.
58th Divisional Artillery.

8th September 1918.

Copies to :-

290th Brigade R.F.A.	1.
291st Brigade R.F.A.	2.
62nd Brigade R.F.A.	3.
108th Army Brigade R.F.A.	4.
63rd Brigade R.F.A.	5.
82nd Brigade R.F.A.	6.
83rd Brigade R.F.A.	7.
113th Heavy Battery.	8.
58th D.A.C.	9.
18th D.A.C.	10.
47th Brigade R.G.A.	11.
58th Division "G".	12.
173rd Infantry Brigade.	13.
174th Infantry Brigade.	14.
175th Infantry Brigade.	15.
R.A., III Corps.	16.
H.A., III Corps.	17.
74th Div. Arty.	18.
21st Div. Arty.	19.
18th Div. Arty.	20.
12th Div. Arty.	21.
Liaison Officer.	22.
R.O.R.A.	23.
Signals Officer, R.A.	24.
War Diary.	25 & 26.
File.	26 & 27.

SEEN BY :-
G.O.C. ....
G.S.O.I ....
G.S.O.II ....
G.S.O.III ....
....

SECRET.   Copy No. 12

58th Divisional Artillery Order No.168.

1. The 173rd Infantry Brigade are attacking EPEHY and PEZIERES tomorrow morning.

2. The First and Final Objectives are shewn in Red, and the line for the 18-pdr. barrage in Black, on attached tracing.

3. After the pause of 10 minutes on the Final Objective as shewn on the tracing, the fire of individual guns will be taken off from the outer flanks at the rate of 100 yards in 5 minutes and placed on the line A.B. upon which, up to 1.0 no Artillery fire will have fallen.
   This line will be kept under fire till 1.20, when all firing will have stopped, and 290th, 62nd, and 108th Army Brigades come directly under the orders of the B.G.C., 173rd Infantry Brigade on their same sections of the Divisional front as before the operation.
   At 1.20, 291st Brigade R.F.A. will stand by ready to fire on any section of the Divisional front under orders from Headquarters, 58th Divisional Artillery.

4. Objectives for 4.5" Hows are shewn in Brown on tracing and will be engaged from 0.0 - 1.20 in bursts of fire.

5. III Corps H.A. are co-operating as shewn in Appendix "A".

6. 58th Divisional Trench Mortars will bombard selected strong points on the road running S.E. through EPEHY and PEZIERES from 0.0 - 0.30 and then stop firing.

7. O.C., 62nd Army Brigade R.F.A. will detail an 18 pounder battery to fire a smoke barrage on the area around X.25.a.0.9, to cover the left flank of our Infantry, from 0.20 till 0.50 being careful to put the M.P.I. well to windward of the railway.

8. 21st Divisional Artillery have been asked to keep the High ground in X.13.d., X.19.a. and b, under fire, and also to put down a smoke barrage between it and on left flank throughout the operation.

9. 113th Heavy Battery will engage targets detailed in Appendix "A".

10. The attack is being carried out by two battalions, and from zero hour onwards a field battery will be placed directly at the disposal of each battalion commander concerned, as follows :-

    Right Battalion by O.C., 291st Brigade R.F.A.
    Left Battalion by O.C., 108th Army Brigade R.F.A.

    In addition a battalion of 174th Infantry Brigade, under orders of B.G.C., 173rd Infantry Brigade is endeavouring to push forward to the railway line in F.1.d. - F.7.b. - F.7.c. and a field battery will be similarly put into action about E.23.d. to support this battalion, by O.C., 290th Brigade R.F.A. and will be at the disposal of the battalion commander concerned.

11. Headquarters 173rd Infantry Brigade and 290th Brigade R.F.A. will move to E.3.a.9.2. about 7.0 p.m. this evening and all orders will be sent there from these Headquarters for distribution. The orderlies indicated in 58th D.A. Order No.156, para.3.(a) of yesterday, will go there accordingly.

- 2 -

12. Lt. Col. W.A.F. Jones, D.S.O., Cdg. 290th Brigade R.F.A. will act as Liaison Officer with B.G.C., 173rd Infantry Brigade.

13. Rates of fire will be Normal throughout.

14. Zero hour is 5.15 a.m. and watches will be synchronised at Headquarters, 290th Brigade R.F.A.

15. ACKNOWLEDGE.

H. Williamson
Major,
Brigade Major, R.A.
58th Divisional Artillery.

9th September 1918.

Copies to :-

290th Brigade R.F.A.	1.
291st Brigade R.F.A.	2.
62nd Brigade R.F.A.	3.
108th Army Brigade R.F.A.	4.
63rd Brigade R.F.A.	5.
82nd Brigade R.F.A.	6.
83rd Brigade R.F.A.	7.
113th Heavy Battery.	8.
58th D.A.C.	9.
18th D.A.C.	10.
47th Brigade R.G.A.	11.
58th Division "G".	12.
173rd Infantry Brigade.	13.
174th Infantry Brigade.	14.
175th Infantry Brigade.	15.
R.A. III Corps.	16.
H.A. III Corps.	17.
74th Div. Arty.	18.
21st Div. Arty.	19.
18th Div. Arty.	20.
12th Div. Arty.	21.
Liaison Officer.	22.
Staff Captain, R.A.	23.
R.O.R.A.	24.
Signals Officer, R.A.	25.
War Diary.	26 & 27.
File.	28 & 29.
58th D.T.M.O.	30.

Appendix "A".

At Zero hour every available How to fire 2 rounds on PEIZERE and EPHY. Then to Zero plus 10 fire on area from W.30.b.8.6. to W.30.d.8.6. and F.1.c.9.9. and F.1.d.1.9.

From Zero plus 10 to Zero plus 20 fire on the Railway Line from X.25.a.0.9. to F.1.b.7.0.

From Zero plus 20 to Zero plus 80 fire on the following points :-

(a) MALASSIAS FARM. F.2.d.1.0.
(b) OLD COPSE. F.9.a.
(c) TETARD WOOD. F.2.a.
(d) Trench from X.25.a. to X.26.d.4.0.

60-pounders.

From zero to zero plus 80, Search and sweep CATELEX VALLEY and DEELISH VALLEY.

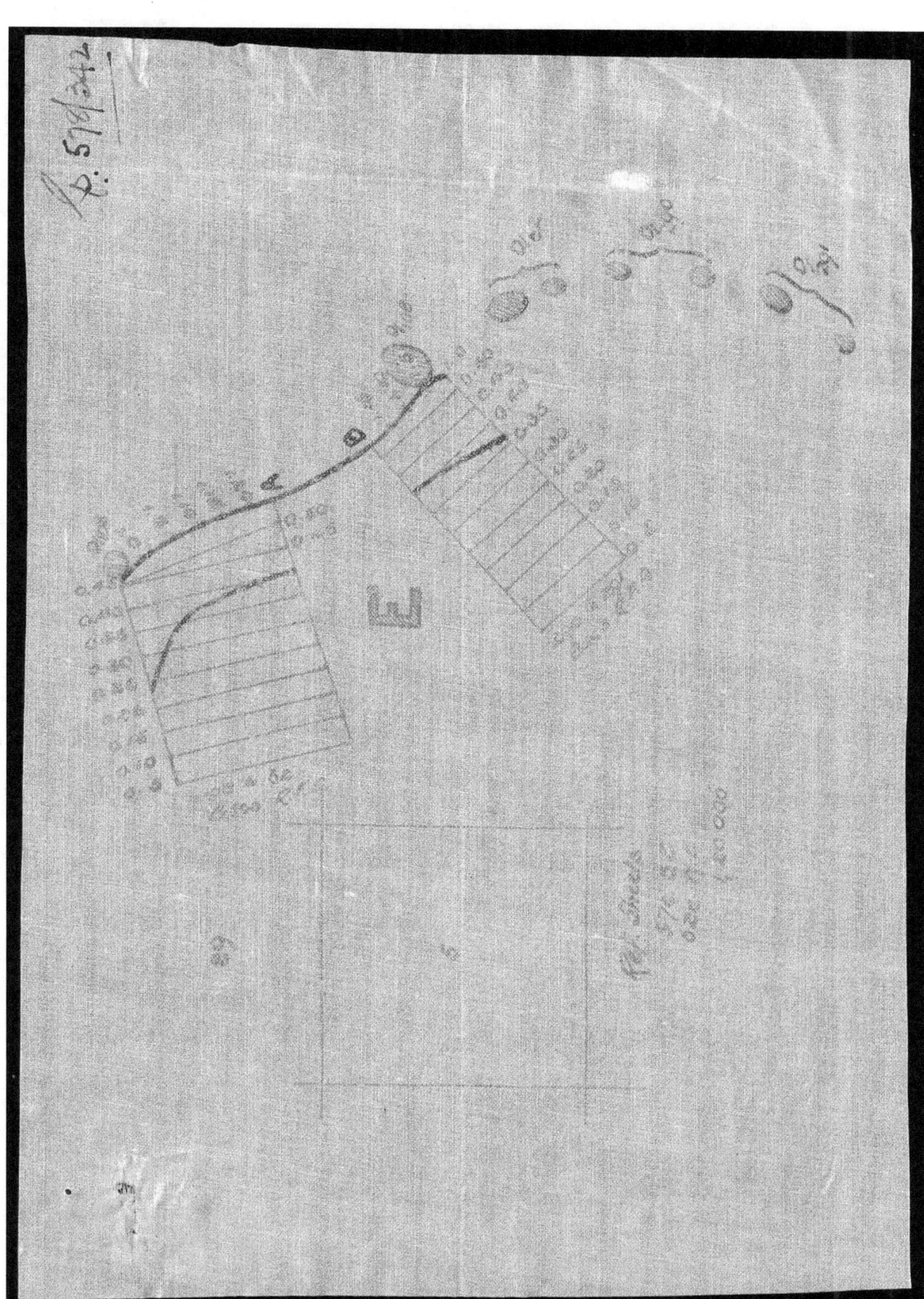

SECRET.

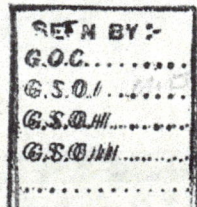

B.M./Y/448.

290th Brigade R.F.A.
291st Brigade R.F.A.
62nd Brigade R.F.A.
63rd Brigade R.F.A.
----

1. Unless the situation materially alters the following artillery reliefs will take place :-

    Night Sept. 12/13th. ~~Cancelled~~

        63rd Brigade R.F.A. relieve 62nd Brigade R.F.A.

    Night Sept. 13/14th.

        291st Brigade R.F.A. relieve 290th Brigade R.F.A.

        All details of relief will be arranged between Brigade Commanders concerned and must not be more than one battery at a time.
        Completion will be wired to this office.

2. ACKNOWLEDGE. *done*

                                    Major,
                                    Brigade Major, R.A.
10th September 1918.   58th Divisional Artillery.

Copies to :-
    58th Division "G".
    R.A., III Corps.
    108 Army Brigade R.F.A.
    58th D.A.C.
    12th Div. Arty.
    Staff Captain, R.A.

290th Brigade R.F.A.
291st Brigade R.F.A.
62nd Brigade R.F.A.
63rd Brigade R.F.A.

Reference this office No.B.M./Y/448 dated 10th September, 1918 -

Night Sept.12/13th.

63rd Brigade R.F.A. relieve 62nd Brigade R.F.A. is cancelled.

Further instructions will be issued direct from III Corps R.A.

Major,
Brigade Major, R.A.
58th Divisional Artillery.

11/9/18.

Copies to :-
58th Division "G".
R.A., III Corps.
108th Army Brigade R.F.A.
58th D.A.C.
12th Div. Arty.
Staff Captain, R.A.

SECRET  Copy No. 11

58th Divisional Artillery Order No.169.

1. Pending a resumption of the offensive, the Divisional front is held by a chain of posts approximately along roads E.12.central and E.12.d. and along the W. edge of EPEHY and PEZIERES.
   There is an organised line of trenches along Sunken road E.12.central - E.12.a. and b. - E.5.b. and d. - W.29.b.& d, which, in case of a hostile counter offensive, will in all probability be the main line of resistance, before actually falling back on the SAULCOURT - GUYENCOURT Ridge.

2. 290th, 62nd and 103th Army Brigades R.F.A. will cover the front as before from South to North, and the 291st Brigade R.F.A. will be in mobile reserve.

3. The 175th Infantry Brigade will hold the line, with Headquarters at E.8.a.5.7, and O.C., 62nd Brigade R.F.A. will get into touch with the B.G.C., and perform duties of Liaison Officer for the three Artillery brigades covering the front. 290th and 103th Army Brigade R.F.A. will make the necessary arrangements for communication with O.C., 62nd Brigade R.F.A. for this purpose.
   O.C., 113th Heavy Battery R.G.A. will also keep in touch with O.C., 62nd Brigade R.F.A.

4. 291st Brigade R.F.A. will reconnoitre positions for the defence of the main line of resistance, mentioned in para.1, at extreme range with H.E. and 106 fuzes, and also O.Ps for observation over the country lying between it and the SAULCOURT - GUYENCOURT Ridge.   continual
   They will keep in touch by orderly with O.C., 62nd Brigade R.F.A. and by telephone with Headquarters, 58th D.A. They will also be prepared to cover a counter-attack on any portion of the Divisional front, to restore the situation should the SAULCOURT - GUYENCOURT Ridge become endangered.

5. O.C., 290th Brigade R.F.A. will detail a battery to be ready to engage a hostile attack down the valley in E.12.central.
   O.C., 62nd Brigade R.F.A. will detail a battery to be ready to engage a hostile attack down the valley E.12.a. - E.6.d.
   These batteries must be well forward, and in such position themselves, or with one section in such a position, that it could engage the objective mentioned from either a half-cock or open position, once the attack was well developed. O.Ps for this purpose must be in close proximity to the guns, or with an organised system of visual communication to them always operating.

6. Group O.Ps for extended views over the area between the present front line and the SAULCOURT - GUYENCOURT Ridge will be established to day by each brigade and manned day and night. Their locations will be reported to this office by wire.

7. Ammunition expenditure will consist of 300 rounds 18-pounder and 50 rounds 4.5" How per brigade, per 24 hours, till further notice except for targets offering exceptional opportunities for killing personnel.

8. All requirements for Liaison Officers for Infantry Battalion Headquarters will be arranged by O.C., 62nd Brigade R.F.A direct.

- 2 -

9. 175th Infantry Brigade are taking over from 173rd Infantry Brigade during the night September 11/12th at an hour which will be notified later, and Liaison duties will pass from O.C., 290th Brigade R.F.A. to O.C., 62nd Brigade R.F.A. at the same hour.

10. ACKNOWLEDGE.

done

H. Williams
Major,
Brigade Major, R.A.
58th Divisional Artillery.

11th September 1918.

Copies to :-
290th Brigade R.F.A.	1.
291st Brigade R.F.A.	2.
108th Army Brigade R.F.A.	3.
62nd Brigade R.F.A.	4.
113th Heavy Battery.	5.
47th Brigade R.G.A.	6.
63rd Brigade R.F.A.	7.
82nd Brigade R.F.A.	8.
83rd Brigade R.F.A.	9.
58th D.A.C.	10.
58th Division "G".	11.
173rd Infantry Brigade.	12.
174th Infantry Brigade.	13.
175th Infantry Brigade.	14.
R.A., III Corps.	15.
H.A., III Corps.	16.
74th Div. Arty.	17.
21st Div. Arty.	18.
12th Div. Arty.	19.
18th Div. Arty.	20.
Liaison Officer.	21.
Staff Captain, R.A.	22.
R.O.R.A.	23.
War Diary.	24 & 25.
File.	26 & 27.

"A" Form.
MESSAGES AND SIGNALS.
Army Form C.2121 (in pads of 100).

TO: 58 Div G

Sender's Number: Y.444
Day of Month: 13

Ref B.M.4/448 dated 10 Sept para 1 is cancelled aaa 291 Bde will not relieve 290 Bde night Sept 13/14th but will remain in mobile reserve pending further instructions aaa 290 Bde will remain in their present position aaa 290 and 291 Bdes to acknowledge aaa Add'd 290 & 291 Bdes rep'd 58 Div G and RA III Corps. aaa

From: 58 D.A.
(sgd) H. Williamson
Major

"A" Form.
MESSAGES AND SIGNALS.

Army Form C.2121 (in pads of 100).

58th (LONDON) DIVISION — This message is on a/c o. Service. GENERAL STAFF — **16 SEP. 1918**

Prefix .... Code .... m.	
Office of Origin and Service Instructions.	

TO — ~~HQ GOC RA~~ 58 Div G.

Sender's Number.	Day of Month.	In reply to Number.	AAA
J.15	16		

Ref BM/4/459 of today aaa Please alter the times to the following aaa 1.0am 1.10am 2.20am 3.0am 3.15am 3.45am 4.15am 4.25am 4.45am 5.0am aaa Added 290 108 & 62 Bdes reptd to GOC RA and 58 Div G.

SENT BY:
GOC ....
G.S.O.1 ....
G.S.O.II ....
G.S.O.III ....

From: 58 D A
Place:
Time:

(Sgd) H Williamson

The above may be forwarded as now corrected. (Z)

Censor. Signature of Addressor or person authorised to telegraph in his name.

B.M./Y/459.

290th Brigade R.F.A.
108th Army Brigade R.F.A.
62nd Brigade R.F.A.

       Gas concentrations will be carried out throughout the night 16/17th Sept. as follows :- each 4.5" Howitzer battery will fire a concentration, 30 rounds, at RAPID rate in accordance with the following programme.

Time	Location
1. am 10.0 p.m.	X.25.a.4.5.
1.10 am 10.20 p.m.	F.2.a.7.5.
2.30 am 10.50 p.m.	F.2.a.2.3.
3 am 11.15 p.m.	X.25.b.8.7.
3.15 am 12.0 midnight	X.26.a.7.3.
3.45 am 12.30 a.m.	X.25.a.4.5.
4.15 am 1.0 a.m.	W.30.b.8.8.
4.25 am 1.45 a.m.	X.25.a.8.0.
4.45 am 2.0 a.m.	F.2.a.7.5.
5 am 2.15 a.m.	X.25.b.8.7.

H Williamson
Major,
Brigade Major, R.A.
58th Divisional Artillery.

16th September, 1918.

Copies to:- 113 Heavy Battery.
            47 Brigade R.G.A.
            58th Division "G".
            R.A., III Corps.

SECRET.

ADDENDUM No.1. to 58th D.A. Order No.170.

1. The positions to be occupied by 63rd and 108th (Army) Brigades R.F.A., for covering the advance of the 173rd Infantry Brigade will be as follows :-

63rd Brigade R.F.A.		108th Army Brigade R.F.A.	
H.Q.	E.3.c.0.8.	H.Q.	E.1.c.2.2.
A/63.	E.4.c.8.8.	A/108.	E.3.c.9.9.
B/63.	E.4.a.6.9.	B/108.	E.3.a.9.1.
C/63.	W.28.b.0.3.	C/108.	E.4.c.2.6.
D/63.	E.3.d.5.5.	D/108.	E.4.c.7.6.

2. These must be occupied and the guns ready to fire by 12 midnight "Y"/"Z" night.

3. Responsibility for the front passes to Os.C. the units which will actually carry out the attack, at 12 midnight on "Y"/"Z" night.

Up to that hour the front held by the 58th Division will be covered as at present - after that hour it will be covered by the 63rd and 108th (Army) Brigades R.F.A., who, in case of a hostile attack will put down a barrage on the line which they are shewn to leave at 0.10 minutes on Tracing "A".

4. The S.O.S. Signal on -

Vth Corps Front is -

GREEN over RED over GREEN.

on the III Corps Front it is -

RED over RED over RED.

5. As soon as the 63rd and 108th (Army) Brigades R.F.A. are in action and ready to fire on "Y"/"Z" night they will wire to this office the code word "CRYSTAL".

6. ACKNOWLEDGE.

H. Williamson
Major,
Brigade Major, R.A.
58th Divisional Artillery.

16th September, 1918.

Copies to all recipients of 58th D.A. Order No.170.

S E C R E T.   Copy No...... 4

58th Divisional Artillery Order No. 170.

1. The 58th Division are attacking PEIZIERES on "Z" day with the 173rd Infantry Brigade.
    The 12th Division are attacking on the Right, and the 21st Division on the Left.
    On arrival at First Objective, see Tracing "A", the 58th Division remain stationary and the 12th and 21st Divisions join hands in front of them and continue the advance.

2. The attack will be covered by a Creeping barrage of 18-pounders and 4.5" Howitzers of the 63rd and 108th (Army) Brigades R.F.A., and a bombardment of strong points by the 85th Brigade R.G.A., which is allotted to the 58th Division for the purpose of the operation.
    Back area bombardments and counter-battery work are being undertaken by III Corps H.A. direct. Targets have been submitted to them and are shewn in Appendix "A".

3. At O.O. the 18-pounder barrage will open at NORMAL rate of fire, equally distributed along the start line over the zones allotted to each brigade in the Tracing "A".
    At O.3. it will creep forward at NORMAL rate. Times of lifting off are shewn at the ends of each line upon which fire is to fall.
    On arrival at the Brown Line marked A.B. each gun will pause for 18 minutes at a SLOW rate, except for the last two minutes when it will fire RAPID and then move forward again at NORMAL rate.
    On arrival at FIRST PROTECTIVE Barrage line the fire of each unit will remain stationary for 5 minutes, after which it will search to a depth of 500^x in bursts of fire for 5 minutes every 15 minutes.
    Each 18-pounder will fire one round of smoke in every 15 rounds, throughout.
    Correctors for shrapnel will be calculated to give 60% on graze.
    Care will be taken that sufficient 106 fuzes are retained for use with H.E. at ranges over 5,000^x.

4. 4.5" Howitzers will conform with the 18-pounder barrage but always keeping 100^x E. of it. When using 106 fuzes they must keep 200^x E. of it.
    They will concentrate their fire in turn on the objectives shewn on attached Tracing "B".

5. At O.190 all fire lifts from FIRST PROTECTIVE Barrage Line and the command of the 63rd and 108th (Army) Brigades R.F.A. passes to the G.R.A., 12th Division, who is issuing all further orders concerning their movements direct to them.
    At O.72, 2-18 pounder batteries of 63rd Brigade R.F.A. come under the orders of C.R.A., 12th Division who will also issue orders direct to them for the application of their fire from that time onwards.
    The direct call on the 85th Brigade R.G.A. passes to C.R.A., 12th Division at the same time as the command of the 63rd and 108th (Army) Brigades R.F.A.

6. 6" Newton Stokes Mortars will co-operate by bombarding the enemy's strong points from zero onwards always keeping at a safe distance E. of the 18-pounder barrage, up to the limits of their range.

7. O.C., 63rd Brigade R.F.A. will detail an officer, not below the rank of Captain, to perform Liaison duties with B.G.C., 173rd Infantry Brigade at E.3.c.7.7., where he will report at 5.0 p.m. on "Y" day, and will be in direct communication with/

with 63rd and 108th (Army Brigades R.F.A.

He will return to his unit when it has been definitely ascertained that the 12th and 21st Divisions have joined hands and are on the 2nd Objective.

8. In the case of a S.O.S. call being received from the air or from the ground during the barrage programme all Artillery Brigades in the Divisional Area affected will at once switch one battery each on to the threatened area for 5 minutes at the rate of 4 rounds per 18-pounder per minute, then for 5 minutes at the rate of 3 rounds per 18-pounder per minute. After 10 minutes the fire will be slowed down and return to the barrage programme as the situation admits.

If the call is near a Divisional boundary the flank brigades will co-operate as detailed above.

9. Calls from the air will be answered as follows:-

(a) During the barrage programme -

LL. Calls.
One 18-pounder and one 4.5" Howitzer battery per brigade to be detailed beforehand for this purpose under brigade arrangements.
Three salvoes will be fired immediately on receipt of the call. If it is repeated after a reasonable interval the bursts will be fired again.

Anti-tank gun.
If any enemy anti-tank gun is observed from the air obviously firing on Tanks and within 1,200 yards from the Tanks it will be reported by the call "LLNF" and answered as for other "LL" Calls.

(b) After completion of the barrage programme -

GF. Calls.
will be answered by a section of all Field and Heavy Artillery batteries that can bring fire to bear.

LL. Calls.
will be answered by all Heavy Artillery batteries in the zone allotted to their Group and all Field Artillery Batteries that can bring fire to bear on the Target with the exception that one 18-pounder battery of each brigade will remain covering the zone allotted to that Brigade.

GF. and LL. Calls.
Three salvoes per battery will be fired immediately on receipt of the call.
If the call is repeated after a reasonable interval these bursts will again be fired.

10. One 18-pounder battery per Brigade will be detailed to engage fleeting targets. They will be the same batteries as those detailed to answer calls from the air.

During the Barrage Programme the fire of these batteries will be superimposed over that of the remainder of the Brigade so that in the event of its being taken off the Barrage no gaps will be left.

The batteries will be in communication with suitable O.Ps.

11./

- 3 -

11. Instructions for defence of the line during the night "Y"/"Z" will be issued separately as an addendum to this order.

12. Watches will be synchronised at H.Q., 173rd Infantry Brigade at 7.15 p.m. on "Y" day.

13. Zero hour and "Z" day will be ~~notified later~~. 5.20 am 18 Sept.

14. H.Q., 12th Divisional Artillery are at D.10.c.5.0.
H.Q., 58th Divisional Artillery will remain at D.22.a.2.4.

15. ACKNOWLEDGE.
done

H. Williamson
Major,
Brigade Major, R.A.
58th Divisional Artillery.

H.Q.R.A.
16/9/18.
T.2.

Copies to:-
63rd Brigade R.F.A.	1. (5)
108th Army Brigade R.F.A.	2. (5)
85th Brigade R.G.A.	3.
18th D.T.M.O.	4.
58th D.T.M.O.	5.
58th D.A.C.	6.
58th Division "G".	7.
173rd Infantry Brigade.	8.
174th Infantry Brigade.	9.
175th Infantry Brigade.	10.
35th Infantry Brigade.	11.
R.A., III Corps.	12.
H.A., III Corps.	13.
12th Div. Arty.	14.
18th Div. Arty.	15.
21st Div. Arty.	16.
74th Div. Arty.	17.
46th Div. Arty.	18.
Staff Captain, R.A.	19.
R.O., R.A.	20.
Signals Officer, R.A.	21.
Liaison Officer.	22.
War Diary.	23. & 24.
File.	25. & 26.

SEEN BY:-
G.O.C.
G.S.O.I ✓
G.S.O.II ✓
G.S.O.III

APPENDIX "A".

Targets for Heavy Artillery have been selected as shewn on attached Tracing "C" and III Corps R.A. have been asked to arrange for these to be engaged on the following lines.

(1). At O.O. every available piece will fire two crashes, on to the village of PEZIERES concentrating on to the selected points.

(2) On completion of (1) Heavy Artillery will lift on to the following objectives :-

(a) Line F.6.a.9.9. - W.30.b.2.0.

(b) Row of houses and road through MC.PHEE POST, MORGAN POST, as far as F.1.a.3.9.

(c) Railway Line and trenches.

(d) Trench Line X.25.b.0.9. X.26.cent. F.2.b.5.8.

(e) Trench Line X.20.c.1.0. X.26.b.2.0. OAK TRENCH, ROOM TRENCH, CHESTNUT AVENUE.

(f) Sunken Road, X.26.b.8.0. - X.21.c.6.0.

(g) Trenches X.21.b.5.0, KILDARE LANE, KILDARE POST, Area X.28.b.7.0. - X.28.b.4.5. - X.28.d.2.8. COTTESMORE TRENCH, CRUCIFORM POST,

(h) CATELEY TRENCH X.28.b.6.5. - X.29.a.8.7. and sunken road.

(i) Trenches X.29.a. and X.30.b. and c.

60 Pounders.

MALASSES ROAD F.3.b.9.9. - X.28.central.

F.2.a.0.8. to Cross roads X.22.c.

CATELEY VALLEY.

These are all lettered on the tracing and they should be engaged up to the last moment it is safe to fire without endangering our Infantry.

In addition fire should be maintained on the railway across the Divisional front from O.O. onwards, and on localities likely to be occupied by the hostile reserves, from the moment that it has to lift off the railway

Other objectives should be engaged as far as possible in depth, so as to ensure that a belt of country at least 500^x deep is continually under fire.

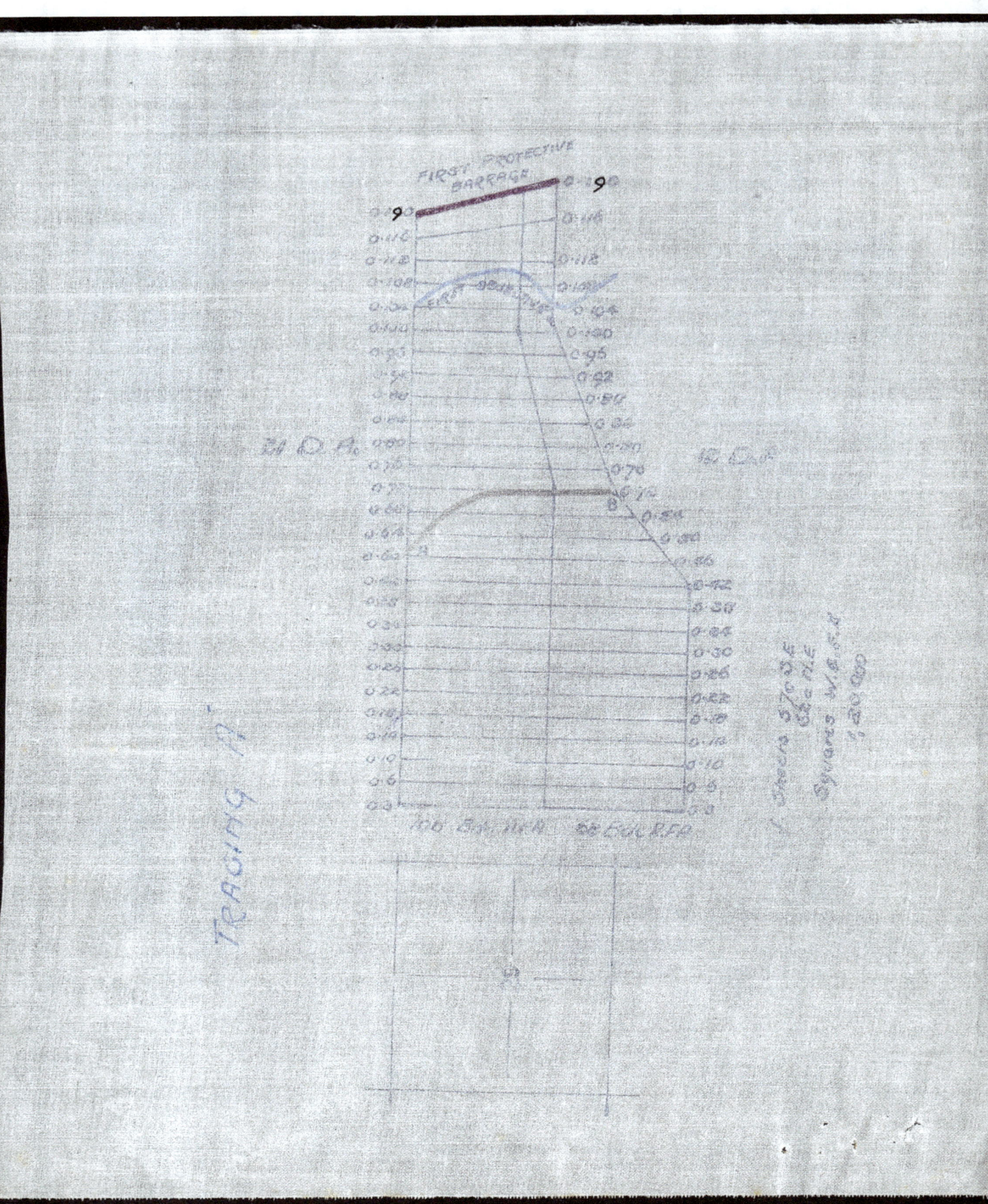

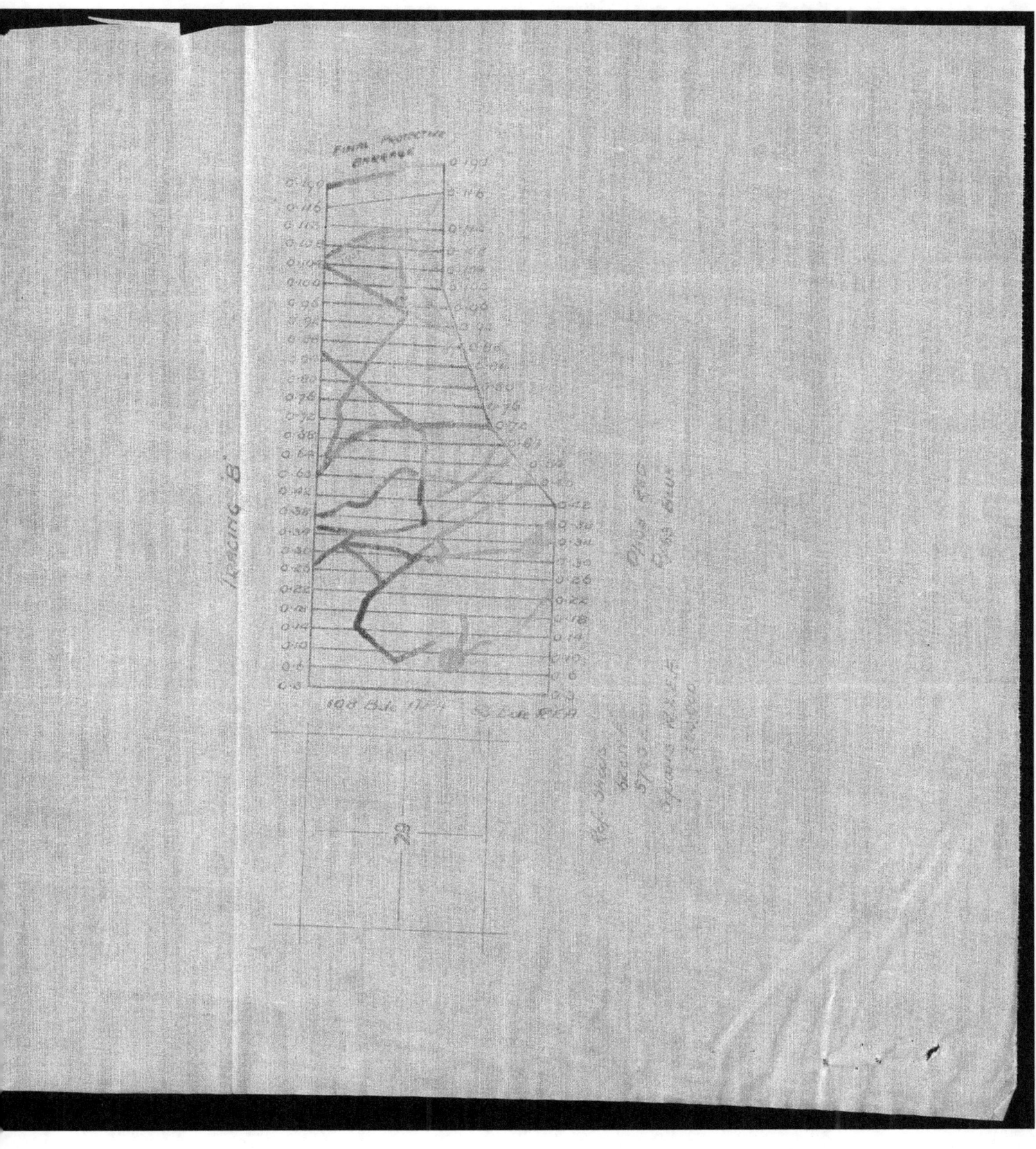

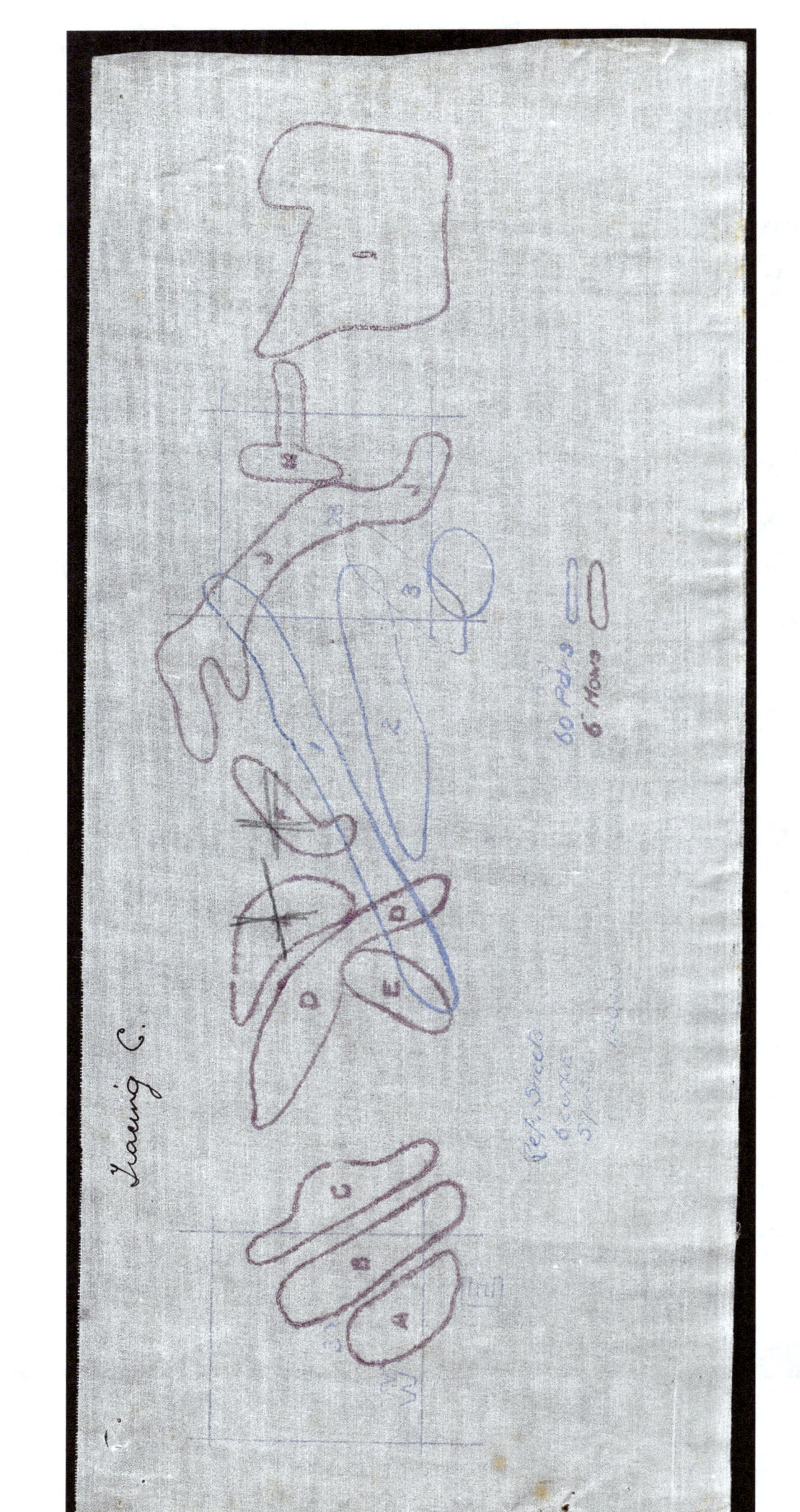

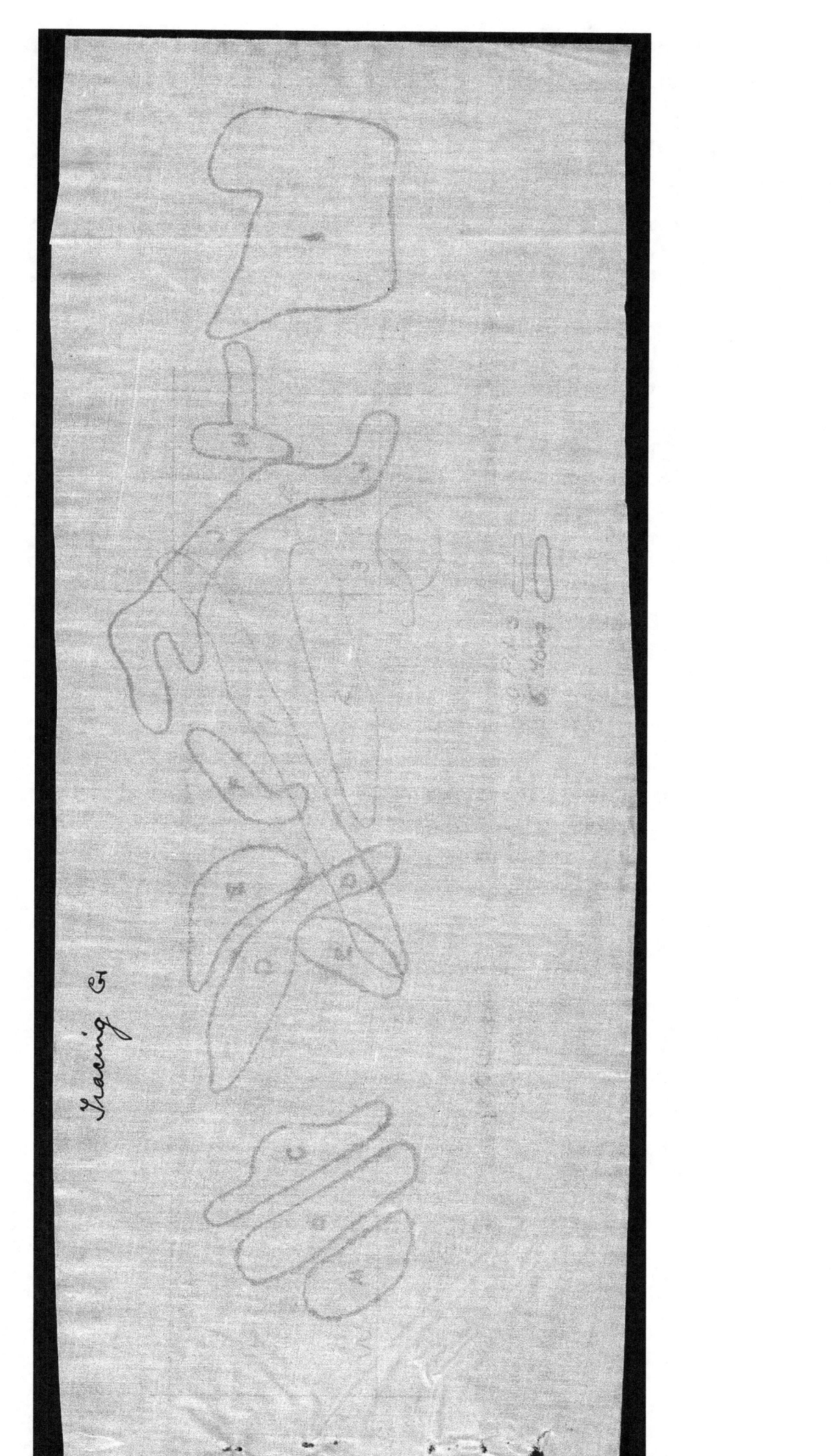

G.S.O.2

Herewith tracing
of H.A. Targets –

A copy of this is
attached to the
order which should
have reached
you by now

[initials]

SECRET. B.M./Y/465.

To all recipients of 58th D.A. Order No.170.

Reference para.13 of 58th D.A. Order No.170 - "Z" day will be 18th September, 1918.
Zero hour will be 5.20 a.m.

ACKNOWLEDGE.

17th September, 1918.

Major,
Brigade Major, R.A.
58th Divisional Artillery.

S E C R E T.

AMENDMENT No.1. to 58th D.A.Order No.170.

Reference Appendix "A" -

Para. 2, sub-para.(a) For "F.6.a.9.9." read "F.1.a.9.9."

                        Major,
               Brigade Major, R.A.
17th Sept.1918.   58th Divisional Artillery.

SECRET.  B.M./Y/466.

290th Brigade R.F.A.
62nd Brigade R.F.A.
108th Army Brigade R.F.A.
----

1. 3 minute concentrations of N.C. will be fired this evening by D/62, D/108, and D/290 in accordance with the following programme. Rates of fire will be RAPID.

5.30 p.m.	X.26.a.4.0.
5.40 p.m.	X.26.b.3.2.
5.50 p.m.	X.25.d.7.7.
6.0 p.m.	X.25.a.3.9.
7.30 p.m.	X.25.c.7.3.
7.40 p.m.	F.2.a.0.8.
8.0 p.m.	F.2.c.5.0.
8.30 p.m.	X.26.c.3.7.
8.45 p.m.	X.26.b.9.0.
9.0 p.m.	X.26.b.2.2.
9.30 p.m.	X.25.c.5.9.
9.45 p.m.	X.25.c.7.4.

   At 10.pm D/108 and D/290 will move to their new positions and D/62 will continue firing gas concentrations of 4 minutes at least 4 times a hour, each at irregular intervals till 5.0 a.m. on the following objectives :-

   X.25.a.4.5.
   X.25.b.8.7.
   X.26.a.6.3.
   X.26.b.8.9.
   F.2.a.2.2.
   F.2.a.7.5.

   62nd and 108th Brigades will synchronise with 290th Brigade R.F.A.

2. Harassing fire over the whole Divisional front will be carried out by 62nd Brigade R.F.A. to avoid the diminuation of guns owing the moves forward being destected by the enemy.

   Ammunition expenditure will be -

   300 rounds per 18 pdr. battery.
   up to 5.15 a.m. September, 18th.

3. All batteries moving to forward positions during the night will fire a small amount of harassing fire from their old ones leaving one gun behind till the last possible moment for that purpose.

   ACKNOWLEDGE.

   Major,
   Brigade Major, R.A.
   58th Divisional Artillery

17th Sept. 1918.

Copy to 58th Div. "G"
173rd Infantry Brigade.

SECRET.   Copy No. 3.

58th Divisional Artillery Order No.171.

1.   The 175th Infantry Brigade are attacking tonight in co-operation with the 33rd Division on the left. Objectives will be –

    33rd Division.   LIMERICK POST.

    58th Division.   (1) KILDARE POST, KILDARE LANE and road running S. to X.28. central.

                                   (2) SPRINT ROAD and DADOS LOOP.

2.   175th Infantry Brigade are forming up on a line running N. and S. through X.27.a.5.9. and will advance at 9.30 p.m.

3.   The attack will be covered by 108th Army Brigade R.F.A. who will bombard the objectives and harass the approaches thereto, throughout the afternoon.
At 9.30 p.m. the bombardment will increase in intensity and forming a standing barrage on the objective.
The South extremity of the 33rd Division barrage is at X.22.c.2.0. from where it lifts at 9.50 p.m. and creeps forward at 100x in 3 minutes till it reaches the S. end of their Protective Barrage at X.23.c.0.7.
The N. extremity of 108th Army Brigade barrage will be at X.22.c.5.0. and the S. end at X.28.b.1.4. It will lift from this line at 10.5. p.m. and subsequent lines upon which fire is to rest, and intervals for them will be communicated direct by 108th Army Brigade R.F.A. by B.G.C., 175th Infantry Brigade.

4.   III Corps H.A. have been asked to bombard the following points throughout the afternoon :-
    BIRD CAGE in X.29.d.
    KILDARE POST and lane S. of it.
    SPRINT ROAD.
    OSSUS WOOD.
At 9.30 p.m. the bombardment on the objectives will be intensified. It will lift off KILLARE POST and lane S. of it at 9.50 p.m. and off SPRINT ROAD at 9.55 p.m., forming a standing barrage on STONE TRENCH and finishing at 10.15 p.m.

5.   An international post is being established with the 33rd Division at X.22.c.5.5. and patrols will be pushed down towards CATELET COPSE to get into touch with 12th Division.

6.   Synchronisation will be done at 175th Infantry Brigade Headquarters.

7.   ACKNOWLEDGE.

                                                     Major,
                                        Brigade Major, R.A.
                                        58th Divisional Artillery.

22nd September, 1918.

Copies to :-
108th Army Brigade R.F.A.
175th Infantry Brigade.
58th Division "G".
R.A., III Corps.
H.A., III Corps.
33rd Div. Artillery.

S E C R E T.

58th Divisional Artillery Order No.172.

1. The 108th Army Brigade R.F.A., now covering the 58th Divisional front will be relieved in action on the morning of September 23rd by the 44th Brigade R.F.A., of 74th D.A.

2. Guides for the Headquarters & batteries of 44th Brigade R.F.A. will be provided by 108th Army Brigade R.F.A. and will meet incoming units at the cross-roads in E.9. central at 10.30 a.m.

3. Units of 108th Army Brigade R.F.A. will proceed immediately relief is completed to the Wagon Lines in E.28.b. and d., vacated by 44th Brigade R.F.A. who will arrange the necessary guides.

4. The Brigade and Battery Commanders of 108th Army Brigade R.F.A. will proceed as early as possible after relief to Headquarters, 74th D.A. at J.11.c.4.1. where they will receive orders. They will then carry out the necessary reconnaissances to enable them to occupy their positions in action on night September 23/24th.

5. The 44th Brigade R.F.A. will take over S.O.S. Lines, Liaison duties, and night and day harassing fire tasks from 108th Army Brigade R.F.A. without any alterations; also all maps, aeroplane photos and intelligence summaries referring to the front which they will cover.

6. 108th Army Brigade R.F.A. will wire to this office amount of ammunition on hand at battery positions and in echelons, on relief.

7. ACKNOWLEDGE.

H. Williamson
Major,
Brigade Major, R.A.
58th Divisional Artillery.

23/9/18.

Copies to:- 108th Army Brigade R.F.A.)
      44th Brigade R.F.A.) For action.
      IIIrd Corps R.A.   )
      IIIrd Corps H.A.   )
      58th Division "G".) For information.
      74th D.A.   )
      175th Inf. Bde.   )

SEEN BY:-
G.O.C. ......
G.S.O.I ......
G.S.O.II ......
G.S.O.III ......

"A" Form.
MESSAGES AND SIGNALS.

No. of Message ....

Prefix .... Code .... m.	Words	Charge	This message is on a/c of	Recd. at .... m.
Office of Origin and Service Instructions.		Sent	**23 SEP. 1918**	Date ....
		At	GENERAL STAFF	From ....
		To		By ....
		By	(Signature of "Franking Officer.")	

TO { 58 Divn "G"

Sender's Number.	Day of Month.	In reply to Number.	A A A
715	23		

Ref D.A.O. 173 para 7 is cancelled aaa Movements of 58 D.A.H.Q. will be notified later

SEEN BY:-
G.O.C. ....
G.S.O.I ....
G.S.O.II ....
G.S.O.III ....

From
Place 58 D.A.
Time

The above may be forwarded as now corrected.

(Z) Sd H Williamson

Censor. Signature of Addressor or person authorised to telegraph in his name.

* This line should be erased if not required.

750,000. W 2186—M509. H. W. & V., Ld. 6/16.

"A" Form.
MESSAGES AND SIGNALS.

Army Form C.2121
(in pads of 100)

Stamp: 58th (LONDON) DIVISION GENERAL STAFF — 23 SEP 1918

TO: 58 Divn G

Sender's Number.	Day of Month.	In reply to Number.	AAA
J16	23		

Ref O.O. 173 para 7 and J15 these Headquarters will remain at D22A2.4 for the present

SEEN BY:-
G.O.C ....
G.S.O.I ✓
G.S.O.II ✓
G.S.O.III ....

From:
Place: 58 D.A.
Time:

SECRET.

58th Divisional Artillery Order No. 173.

1. The 12th Division are relieving the 58th Division in the line tonight, September 23/24th.
Command passes on completion of relief.

2. Command of 44th Brigade R.F.A., now covering the sector of the front held by the 58th Division, passes from C.R.A., 58th Division to C.R.A., 12th Division on completion of the Infantry relief and will be notified to this office by wire.

3. O.C., 44th Brigade R.F.A. will get into immediate touch with O.C., 63rd Brigade R.F.A. whose Headquarters are at E.4,c.6.5., and under whom he will be grouped when the 12th Division take over.

4. The 58th Division 6" Newton Stokes Mortar Battery now in PEZIERES will be withdrawn today and both batteries will concentrate in LIERAMONT where they will receive orders for their further moves.
The amount of ammunition and location of dumps left behind by them will be wired to this office.

5. The S.A.A. Section, 58th D.A.C. will remain under the orders of 58th Division.

6. At 10.0 a.m. September 25th the 58th Divisional Artillery complete (less S.A.A. Section, 58th D.A.C.) passes to the command of the Australian Corps and will cover the 27th American Division, under orders which are being issued by G.O.C., R.A. Australian Corps.

7. Cancelled. Headquarters, 58th Divisional Artillery close at D.22.a.2 and reopen at VAUX WOOD, about U.29.a., at 11.0 a.m. Sept. 24th.

8. ACKNOWLEDGE.
done.

23/9/18

H. Williamson
Major,
Brigade Major, R.A.
58th Divisional Artillery.

Copies to:-
44th Brigade R.F.A.	1.	R.A., III Corps.	11.		
63rd Brigade R.F.A.	2.	H.A., III Corps.	12.		
290th Brigade R.F.A.	3.	R.A., Aust. Corps.	13.		
291st Brigade R.F.A.	4.	H.A., Aust. Corps.	14.		
58th D.A.C.	5.	58th Division "G"	15.		
58th D.T.M.O.	6.	58th Division "Q"	16.		
12th Div. Arty.	7.	27th Amer. Division.	17.		
33rd Div. Arty.	8.	175th Inf. Brigade.	18.		
18th Div. Arty.	9.	Staff Captain, R.A.	19.		
74th Div. Arty.	10.	R.O.R.A.	20.		
		Signals Officer, R.A.	21.		
		War Diary and File.	22 - 25.		

SEEN BY:-
G.O.C.
G.S.O.I.
G.S.O.II.
G.S.O.III.

October 1918

Place	Date	Hour	Summary
H.Q.R.A. D.22.a.2.4.	1st	—	H.Q.R.A. resting at D.22.a.2.4. 290th Brigade R.F.A. in action under 3rd Australian Div. with H.Q. F.21.a.95.65. "A" Bty. F.23.b.25.55 B/290 F.23.b.25.30 C/290 F.23.b.1.0 D/290 F.23.b.12.18. 291st Brigade R.F.A. in action also under 3rd Australian D.A. H.Q. at F.21.d.40.40, A/291 F.17.c.70.40 B/291 F.17.d.10.10 C/291 F.23.b.35.90 D/291 F.23.a.95.10
D.22.a.2.4.	2nd	9 a.m.	Both Brigades moved forward under the 5th D.A. (Australian) 290th Bde. with H.Q. at A.20.b.1.8. A/290 A.14.c.75.75 B/290 A.21.a.4.9. A/290 A.15.c.3.8. C/290 A.15.c.3.4. and 291st Bde. R.F.A. D/290 A.27.a.5.0. A/291 A.27.d.7.7. B/291 A.27.c.5.5. C/291 A.27.d.6.9. D/291 A.27.d.3.5. The enemy still hold LE CATELET on the North but have retired from BONY and our line now runs considerably East of this Village.
	4th	6 pm	Batteries and Brigades moved froward again to positions as follows:— 290th Bde. H.Q. A.9.b.7.7. A/290 S.28.c.8.8. B/290 S.28.c.2.6. C/290 S.29.c. D/290 A.4.a.5.3. 291st Bde. R.F.A. H.Q. A.5.c.4.7. A/291 A.12.c.7.3. B/291 A.12.d.3.4. C/291 A.12.d.5.4. D/291 A.12.c.4.5. and fired due North from these positions.
	5th/6th 7th/8th		Brigades moved up to positions North and East of GOUY and Wagon Lines moved up also. H.Q.R.A. moved to advanced H.Q. in the HINDENBURG LINE South of BONY at A.21.a.7.7. at 11 a.m. and took over command of 290th and 291st Brigades R.F.A. who supported the attack of the 151st Brigade 50th Division with the 58th Division, V Corps, on their Left, and the 66th Division XIII Corps, on their Right. Zero hour was 1 a.m. and 5.10 a.m. Both attacks were a complete success and at 6 p.m. we had orders that the Brigades and our H.Q. could pull out to the LONGAVESNES Area.
	9th		H.Q.R.A. returned to GURLU WOOD and 290th and 291st Bdes. to their old Wagon Lines around AIZECOURT and SAULCOURT.
HERSIN - COUPIGNY CHATEAU.	10th 11th		H.Q. and Brigades packed up for tomorrow's march and entrainment. 290th Bde. R.F.A. entrained at TINCOURT for HERSIN; also T.M. Batteries and Sections of D.A.C. 291st Bde. R.F.A., H.Q. D.A.C. H.Q.R.A. entrained at PERONNE for BULLY GRENAY.
	12th		The latter unit entrained at midnight and left at 12.50 a.m.; arrived at BULLY GRENAY at 4.30 p.m. but were not allowed to detrain until 7.30 p.m. After watering and feeding, the H.Q. marched to the CHATEAU at HERSIN-COUPIGNY which was reached at 1.30 a.m. Moved again at 9.0 a.m. to MAROC with H.Q. 24th Division. C.R.A. took over from C.R.A. 24th Division at 2 p.m.
MAROC	13th		

Army Form C. 2118.

WAR DIARY
INTELLIGENCE SUMMARY

Page 2.

(Erase heading not required.)

Instructions regarding War Diaries and Intelligence
Summaries are contained in F.S. Regs. Part II.
and the Staff Manual respectively. Title pages
will be prepared in manuscript.

Place	Date	Hour	Summary of Events and Information	Remarks and references to Appendices
	14th/16th. 17th 18th		at 2 p.m. as follows :- The Infantry held a line bounded on the South by a line O.23.cent. - P.14.cent. - P.15.b.1.9. and Northern boundary the SOUCHEZ DEULE CANAL (incl) (Sheet 36C or 44 A.) held by 174th Infy. Brigade with 242nd Army Bde. R.F.A. in support. The 173rd Infy. Bde. with 48th Army Bde. R.F.A. covering them, forming a defensive flank between 174th Infy. Bde.; Left Flank and 15th Division's Right Flank about ANNAY. The 175th Infy. Bde. supported the 174th Infy. Bde. 169th Army Bde. R.F.A. covers whole Divisional Front directly under the orders of C.R.A. 58th Division. 290th and 291st Bdes. R.F.A. resting at HERSIN and BULLY GRENAY respectively. Steady advance continued with Artillery in close support. Many rires in enemy back areas. H.Q.R.A. moved to O.23.b.5.6. (LA TOUR MALAKOF) in MONTIGNY at 11 a.m. 290th Bde. R.F.A. moved from HERSIN to billets in MONTIGNY and relieved the 169th Army Bde. R.F.A. in Divisional Reserve on the 19th. 291st Bde. R.F.A. marched to billets in and around DOURGIES and relieve 48th Army Bde. R.F.A. in the line on the 19th.	
ERSEE	19th		H.Q.R.A. moved to BERSEE at 5 p.m. Our line now runs Approx. A.30.b.0.0. - B.1.c.cent. - B.7.cent. - along road in H.13.b. and c. to H.13.c.c.0. (CARDONNERIE) Brigades were as follows :- 291st Bde. R.F.A. relieved the 48th Army Bde. R.F.A. in and around RUE COLETTE (L.31.) 242nd Army Bde. R.F.A. are following up the advance on the left flank in the neighbourhood of LE PARADIS in L.25.a. 290th Bde. R.F.A. moved up from HARNES to MONCHEAUX Area. By nightfall, our line ran H.19.a.0.0. - H.7.d.2.2. - H.7.b.b.0. - H.1.c.5.7. - A.30.d.1.8. A Section each from 23rd Siege Battery R.G.A. and 308th Siege Battery R.G.A. (6" Hows) are being pushed well forward in support of the Advanced Guard. The advance was continued at dawn and by dark our troops were on the line H.18.b.0.0. - B.17.b.0.0. - having met with scarcely any opposition. The Brigades moved and were to be found as follows :- 291st Bde. R.F.A. (Right Bde. with 175th Infy. Bde.) around AIX (H.16.b.) with advanced battery at H.11.d.3.2. and 242nd Army. Bde. R.F.A. at H.3.c.5.7. (Left Bde. with 173rd Infy. Bde. H.Q.) and a forward battery at B.29.b.7.0. 290th Bde. R.F.A. in Divisional Reserve near VERT BOIS and LE CHATELET Area (B.13. and 14)	
	20th			
AY	21st.		H.Q.R.A. moved to CHATEAU at LANNAY (H.3.c.5.7.) and the Brigades were at the following locations :- 291st Bde. R.F.A. I.4.d.8.6. 242nd Army Bde. R.F.A. I.4.a.5.5. 290th Bde. R.F.A. at AIX. The 58th D.A.C. are also at LANNAY.The Sections of 6" Hows. are /	

58th Divl. Arty.

WAR DIARY
INTELLIGENCE SUMMARY.
(Erase heading not required).

Page 3.

Army Form C. 2118.

Place	Date	Hour	Summary of Events and Information	Remarks and references to Appendices
LANNAY.	21st.		are at I.2.b. and I.15.R. RUE MOLIERE. I.18.b.0.0. RONGY - LESDAIN - JOLLAIN - MERLAIN Car line at nightfall ran as follows :- I.18.b.0.0. RONGY - LESDAIN - JOLLAIN - MERLAIN on our Divisional Front. This line was exploited to the East but the CANAL was not quite reached.	
	22nd.		The 173rd Infy. Bde. attempt to cross the CANAL at ESPAIN but were unsuccessful. Sections of the 23rd Siege and 308th Siege Batteries R.G.A. came under direct control of G.R.A. 58th Division.	
	23rd.		No change in dispositions of Brigades in line. 290th Bde. R.F.A. made reconnaissances for forward positions. Forward Section of C/291 at I.11.c.50.80 had five horses killed by a gas shoot. No changes in dispositions.	
	24th.		Brigades were located as follows :- 242nd Army Bde. R.F.A., with 173rd Infy. Bde., H.Q. I.2.b.3.2. Batteries in C.22.c., C.30.cent. C.28.b. and B.A.C. at B.30.d.3.5. 23rd Siege Battery Section of 6" Hows. I.4.a.2.9. With 175th Infy. Bde. 291st Bde. R.F.A. H.Q. I.4.d.8.6. and batteries at I.16.a., I.15.b., I.11.c., forward Sections of C and D Bttys. I.9... Section of 60-pounders replaced the 308th Battery 6" Hows. and came into action at I.8.a.9.7. 290th Bde. R.F.A. were in Divisional Reserve at AIX. H.Q.R.A., D.A.C., and D.T.M.O. at LANNAY.	
	25th.		At 3 p.m., the enemy blew and evacuated the FORT de MAULDE and our patrols are in close touch.	
	26th.		As a result of yesterday's advance, the 291st Bde. R.F.A. occupied positions as follows - which had previously been under observation from the FORT de MAULDE. H.Q. (unchanged) I.4.d.8.6. A/291 I.17.b.3.7. B/291 I.11.b.5.2. C/291 I.10.b.4.4. D/291 I.17.b.9.5. The Section of 60-pounders did not move. By nightfall, our troops were on the Railway Line East of MAULDE, the enemy having withdrawn East of the River.	
	27th.		The K90th Bde. R.F.A. relieved the 291st. Bde. R.F.A., the latter occupying the billets and area in AIX vacated by the 290th Bde. R.F.A. Relief was completed at 4.40 p.m. and positions of 290th Bde. R.F.A. are as follows :- H.Q. I.4.d.8.6. A/290 I.17.b.3.7. with forward guns at J.21.a.35.66 and J.21.b.25.50 so placed as to enfilade the streets in FLINES LEZ MORTAGNE. B/290 4 guns at I.11.b.5.2. and enfilade gun at J.13.d.1.7. C/290 I.11.c.8.3. D/290 I.11.d.5.1 The Section of 60-pounders at I.8.a.9.7.	
	28th.		The Section of 60-pounders moved forward to C.22.d.00.30., in the morning. Situation very /	

Army Form C. 2118.

WAR DIARY
or
INTELLIGENCE SUMMARY

Page 4.

(Erase heading not required.)

Instructions regarding War Diaries and Intelligence Summaries are contained in F. S. Regs., Part II. and the Staff Manual respectively. Title pages will be prepared in manuscript.

Place	Date	Hour	Summary of Events and Information	Remarks and references to Appendices
	29th		very quiet. No hostile shell fire or gas shelling reported. B/242 moved forward to I.6.a.8.5. with forward gun at J.1.a.1.9.	
	30th		B/290 moved forward to J.15.d.1.7. Very quiet day. E.A. dropped many pamphlets at RUMEGIES.	
	31st		Infantry Line now runs South to North J.10.c.2.2. - road in J.10.c. to LE FORT - Post at J.9.b.9.2. - thence along line of railway at J.9.a.5.7. and CANAL to D.19.b.5.3. One at Sugar Factory.	

31st October 1918.

[signature]

Brigadier General,
C.R.A., 58th Division.

Army Form C. 2118.

WAR DIARY
or
INTELLIGENCE SUMMARY

(Erase heading not required.) Headquarters, 58th Divisional Artillery. Nov./1918.

Instructions regarding War Diaries and Intelligence Summaries are contained in F.S. Regs., Part II. and the Staff Manual respectively. Title pages will be prepared in manuscript.

No 23

Place	Date	Hour	Summary of Events and Information	Remarks and references to Appendices
			November, 1918.	
LANNAY.	1st.		No change in the situation or locations of batteries which are as follows :- With 174th Inf. Bde.	
H.3.b.80.20.			H.Q., QUESNOY, 290th Brigade R.F.A. Group H.Q., I.4.d.80.60. A/290, J.21.a.40.60, B/290, J.13.c. & d. C/290, I.17.b.40.55, D/290. J.20.c.80.90, B/242, I.6.a. with enfilade gun at D.25.c.50.30. D/242, G.22.c.45.80. Section of 60 pdrs. (108 H.B.) C.22.d.00.30. Section 6" Hows. (23rd S.B.) I.4.a.20.90. The 291st Brigade R.F.A. in divisional reserve around AIX and H.Q.242 (Army) Bde. R.F.A. with A & C. Batteries at HOWARDRIES and RUMEGIES.	
	2nd.		Forward positions were reconnoitred and chosen as follows C/290 Bty, I.14.c.20.70. H.Q., 291st Brigade R.F.A. RONGY, "A" Battery, C.30.a.10.50, "B" Battery, C.30.b.20.20, "C" Battery, I.6.b.30.60. "D" Battery, J.1.a.20.80. A/242, C.30.a.80.20. C/242, C.30.a.00.60. D/242, C.30.c.80.90. The necessary range required being 600 yards east of the general line MINES - ROEUX - SART COLIN can be reached by all other batteries from their present position should the line advance. Zones of fire are allotted as follows :- 290th Brigade R.F.A. East & West Grid through K.7.a.0.0. East & West Grid through E.25.a.0.0. 242nd Army Brigade R.F.A. E & W. Grid through E.25.a.0.0. E & W. grid through E.13.a.0.0. 291st Brigade R.F.A. superimposed over whole front.	
LANNAY	3/6th.		No change on the front, little shelling reported and this chiefly gas shelling. On the 4th	

T.131. Wt. W708-776. 500000. 4/15. Sir J. C. & S.

Army Form C. 2118.

WAR DIARY
or
INTELLIGENCE SUMMARY.
(Erase heading not required.)

Instructions regarding War Diaries and Intelligence Summaries are contained in F.S. Regs., Part II. and the Staff Manual respectively. Title pages will be prepared in manuscript.

- 2 -

Place	Date	Hour	Summary of Events and Information	Remarks and references to Appendices
	7th	6.30am.	The Divisional T.Ms moved up to RONGY. Weather very wet. At this hour the enemy retired from his positions on the east bank of the Canal - ESCAULT River. Close touch was maintained by our troops and artillery fire was brought to bear on many suitable targets. No artillery could cross the canal or river. Our patrols by nightfall were on eastern outskirts of LAPLAIGNE - MORTAGNE. 58th D.T.M.O. with "X" & "Y" Batteries remained in RONGY. H.Q.242nd Army Brigade R.F.A. and A & C Batteries withdrawn from action to their Wagon Lines at I.2.b.60.45. I.7.d.80.60, and H.5.d.90.90 respectively.	
	8th.		The advance was continued by 175th Infantry Brigade with 291st Brigade R.F.A. on the right, and 174th Infantry Brigade with 290th Brigade R.F.A. with B & D Batteries, 242nd Army Brigade R.F.A. attached, on the left. By night the line FLINES-LES-MORTAGNE - ROEUX - SART COLIN was reached.	
BLEHARIES	9th.		H.Q.R.A. moved to BLEHARIES. D.T.M.O. and all personnel joined D.A.C. for duty the equipment being dumped at RONGY. The advance continued, no opposition being encountered, the batteries did not come into action but moved with the main body of infantry except the forward batteries detailed to accompany the advance guard. At 8 p.m. the Divisional line ran PERUWELZ (inclusive) - thence along main road east of ROUCOURT and BURY to road junction	

WAR DIARY
or
INTELLIGENCE SUMMARY.
(Erase heading not required.)

Army Form C. 2118.

Instructions regarding War Diaries and Intelligence Summaries are contained in F.S. Regs., Part II. and the Staff Manual respectively. Title pages will be prepared in manuscript.

- 3 -

Place	Date	Hour	Summary of Events and Information	Remarks and references to Appendices
WIERS.	10th.		at F.4.c.10.60. 173rd Infantry Brigade and 242nd Army Brigade RFA. remaining in present present location. H.Q. 290th Brigade R.F.A. E.15.c.40.90. and H.Q. 291st Brigade RFA. WIERS. The advance was continued no alteration taking place in the artillery arrangements. No opposition was met and by nightfall the H.Qs. were as follows. H.Q.R.A., WIERS, 290th Brigade R.F.A. BELOEIL, 291st Brigade R.F.A. ECACHERIES, with their batteries around B.29. H.Q. 242nd Army Brigade R.F.A. HOWARDRIES (no move) D.A.C. LA CROIX.	
BELOEIL.	11th.		H.Q.R.A. moved to BELOEIL and 58th D.A.C. to GRANDGLISE (G.6.c.50.30). Hostilities ceased at 11 a.m. and troops remained on the line reached at that hour. Brigades were as follows :- 290th Brigade R.F.A. GROSAGE, 291st Brigade R.F.A. ECACHERIES and batteries withdrew to their wagon lines. D.A.C. at GRANDGLISE.	
	12/17th.		No moves. Units cleaned up and carried out usual parades as for rest.	
	17th.		290th Brigade R.F.A., H.Q. & B & C Batteries moved to QUEVAUCAMPS, A & D batteries to BLATON.	
PERUWELZ	21st.		291st Brigade R.F.A. moved back to area of WIERS with C Battery at CALONELLE and D Bty at LA CROIX.	
	22nd.		H.Q.R.A. moved to PERUWELZ where Divisional H.Q. are now billetted.	
	23/28th.		No change in locations.	

Army Form C. 2118.

WAR DIARY
or
INTELLIGENCE SUMMARY.
(Erase heading not required.)

Instructions regarding War Diaries and Intelligence Summaries are contained in F.S. Regs., Part II. and the Staff Manual respectively. Title pages will be prepared in manuscript.

Place	Date	Hour	Summary of Events and Information	Remarks and references to Appendices
PERUWELZ.	29th.		291st Brigade R.F.A. moved to better billets for men and horses in BELOEIL.	
	21/30th.		Education for post bellum employ being arranged for during morning and football and athletics during the afternoon.	
			Educational classes are being well attended.	

[signature]

Brigadier General,
C.R.A., 58th Division.

SECRET.   Copy No. .....

58th Divisional Artillery Operation Order No. 186.

1. The 58th Division is under orders to force the passage of the ESCAUT at 48 hours notice.
   "Z" Day and Zero Hour will be notified later.
   The 15th Division on the left flank will also be attacking, and the 52nd Division on the right have been asked to make a demonstration.

2. The operation is being carried out by the 174th Infantry Brigade on the Right and the 175th Infantry Brigade on the Left.

   Divisional Boundaries are as follows :-

   South.

   K.13.a.3.5. - K.19.b.8.7. - K.15.a.5.0. along S. bank of River LA VERGNE - K.12.d.8.8. - L.7.b.0.0. - L.3.c.0.0. - L.4.c.0.5 - L.12.a.9.9.

   Inter-Brigade.

   J.2.b.0.0 - D.28.b.0.0 - D.29.a.0.4. thence due East.

   North.

   D.20.a.3.7. - D.12.c.0.0. - E.10.c.0.0. - E.11.c.8.3. - F.4.a.0.0. - F.5.a.0.5. - thence due East

3. The Infantry will be crossing the River by rafts and pontoons in as many places as possible but confined to the following localities :-

   J.10.b.   J.9.b.   J.3.d.   D.26.a.   D.19.d.

   Artillery pontoon bridges will be constructed as soon as possible at MORTAGNE and ESPAIN.

4. The Final Objective of the Infantry will be the approximate line FLINES LES MORTAGNES - ROEUX - SART COLIN, which will be consolidated.

5. The Field Artillery available to cover the operation will be grouped as follows :-

   Covering 174th Infantry Brigade.

   RIGHT GROUP.   (Lt. Col. W.A.F. JONES, D.S.O.)

       290th Brigade R.F.A.
       108th Army Brigade R.F.A.

   Covering 175th Infantry Brigade.

   LEFT GROUP.   (Lt. Col. R. LONGSTAFF, D.S.O.)

       291st Brigade R.F.A.
       242nd Army Brigade R.F.A.

   Orders referring to the artillery distribution and action after the capture of the final objective will be issued later, but all batteries covering the attack will be able to reach a line 600 yards East of it for protective purposes, without moving forward.

6. The /

6. The Infantry are endeavouring to cross the River just before dawn without any supporting fire. This will open at Zero Hour, by which time they are expected to be established East of the River, in sufficient strength to capture the first line of villages as soon as the barrage lifts off them.

   Details of successive objectives and the times at which fire lifts off them are given separately in Appendix "A" and Tracings issued therewith.

7. Smoke Barrages on selected areas will be fired from 0.0 onwards by the 4.5" Howitzers. These and the other tasks allotted to 4.5" Howitzers are shewn in Appendix "B".

   One Smoke shell in every ten ordinary shell will also be fired by all 18-pounders from 0.0 until the available supply is exhausted.

8. "X" and "Y" Trench Mortar Batteries will put 8 - 6" Newton Mortars into action to bombard selected points from 0.0 onwards.

   Locations and Tasks are shewn in Appendix "C".

9. The Heavy Artillery specially allotted to cover the attack consists of 5 - 8" Howitzers and 11 - 6" Howitzers of the 30th Brigade R.G.A. and 2 - 60-pounders 108th Heavy Battery R.G.A.

   Tasks for the Heavy Artillery are shewn in Appendix "D".

10. The greatest secrecy and care is to be observed in the preparation for these operations.

    The Field Artillery Batteries not at present in action will occupy their positions on Y/Z night, but the 6" Newton Mortars will be put into action immediately.

    Instructions with regard to ammunition to be dumped are issued separately. Appendix "E".

    This must not commence before the night X/Y.

11. Previous instructions with regards to Artillery detailed to cross the River first are cancelled, and O's C. RIGHT and LEFT GROUPS will each detail 1 Section of 18-pounders and 1 Section 4.5" Hows. to cross as soon as the necessary bridges are completed.

    These will only be used for close support of the attacking infantry after they have made good the line MORTAGNE - LA PLAIGNE - CIN and are advancing on their final objective. They should not be sent across prematurely.

    They must be supplied with every known device for making a rapid and efficacious platform, as the ground will be extremely marshy. Otherwise they should travel as light as possible.

12. Each Field Artillery Brigade will man a Brigade Observation Post (in addition to the battery ones) W. of the CANAL, and also despatch an officers patrol with the Infantry to keep in touch with the situation.

    Instructions with reference to communications are issued separately. Appendix "F".

13. Artillery Group Commanders will establish their Headquarters as close as possible to those of the Infantry Brigades which they /

3.

13 contd.
they cover. If required, they will remain with the B.G.'s C. Infantry Brigades throughout the operation.
Battalion Liaison Officers will <u>not</u> be supplied, but at least two battery patrols per Brigade will be sent forward in addition to the Brigade patrol to keep in touch with the situation.

14. At least 48 hours notice will be given before Zero Day.

15. ACKNOWLEDGE.

N. /11/18.

Major,
Brigade Major, R.A.,
58th Divisional Artillery.

Distribution.

290th Bde. R.F.A.	1 (5)	R.A., Ist Corps.	15	
291st Bde. R.F.A.	2 (5)	H.A., Ist Corps	16	
242nd Army Bde. R.F.A.	3 (5)	12th Div. Arty.	17	
108th Army Bde. R.F.A.	4 (5)	15th Div. Arty.	18	
58th D.A.C.	5	Staff Captain R.A.	19	
D.T.M.O.	6 (3)	R.O.R.A.	20	
108th Heavy Btty. R.G.A.	7	R.A. Signals Officer	21	
23rd Siege Battery	8	War Diary	22	23
30th Bde. R.G.A.	9 (5)	File	24	25
46th Bde. R.G.A.	10			
58th Division "G"	11			
173rd Infy. Bde.	12			
174th Infy. Bde.	13			
175th Infy. Bde.	14			

APPENDICES.

A. Tasks for 18-pounders, with Tracings.

B. Smoke Screens for 4.5" Howitzers, and subsequent Tasks.

C. Tasks for 6" Newton Stokes Mortars.

D. Tasks for Heavy Artillery.

E. Ammunition to be dumped at positions.

F. Instructions for Communications.

APPENDIX "B".

SMOKE SCREEN and other Tasks for 4.5" Howitzers.

1. D/108

    (a)   0.0   2 4.5" Hows. (SMOKE) on FORT de FLINES till

        These two Howitzers will mix B.C.G. with their Smoke Shell in 4-minute concentrations at a time. This must fall <u>in</u> the FORT, but the Smoke Screen must obscure the view to the West and North.

        Approx. Expenditure. 200 B.S.
                               100 B.C.G.

        1 4.5" How. lift on to J.12.b.7.2. with H.E.)
        1 4.5" How. lift on to J.12.a.8.5. with H.E.)

                                             till

    (b)   0.0   4 4.5" Hows. (SMOKE) on J.5.d.4.6. - J.4.b.0.0. SMOKE   till O.

        This Smoke Screen must prohibit observation of MORTAGNE and FLINES from the ground in J.4.b. and J.5.a.

        Approx. expenditure. 320 B.S.

    O.   Lift as follows
        1 How.   J.12.a.3.9.
        1 How.   J.6.c.5.7.
        1 How.   J.6.a.7.3.
        1 How.   J.30.d.1.2.
        all with H.E.

2. D/290.

    (a)   0.0   2 4.5" Hows. (H.E.) on J.11.a.9.9   till

        Lift on to J.5.a.8.2.   till

        Lift on to J.6.a.2.3.   till

        Lift on to K.1.a.2.4.   till

    (b)   0.0   2 4.5" Hows. (H.E.) on J.4.c.9.5.   till

        Lift on to D.29.c.2.2.   till

        Lift on to J.6.a.2.8.   till

        Lift on to E.25.d.3.3.   till

    (c)   0.0   1 4.5" How. (H.E.) on D.26.b.7.9.   till

        Lift on to D.28.d.6.5.   till

        Lift on to D.30.b.3.3.   till

    (d) /

2.

  (d) 0.0 1 4.5" How. (H.E.) on D.20.b.8.2. till

       Lift on to D.29.a.2.2.   till

       Lift on to D.24.c.8.2.   till

3. <u>D/291.</u>

   0.0   6 4.5" Hows. (SMOKE) on J.4.c.0.8. –
        D.27.d.0.0   till

    This Smoke Screen is to smother the enemy's
    wire and defences in this area and to
    obscure the troops attacking MORTAGNE
    from the LA PLAIGNE Area.

       <u>Estimated expenditure</u> 170 B.S.

   Lift as follows

  (a) 2 4.5" Hows. (H.E.) on to D.27.b.0.8. till

  (b) 2 4.5" Hows. (H.E.) on to D.28.a.5.5. till

  (c) 2 4.5" Hows. (H.E.) on to D.21.d.8.1. till

   Lift as follows

  (a) 2 4.5" Hows on to D.22.b.2.2. till

  (b) 2 4.5" Hows. on to D.22.a.3.8. till

  (c) 2 4.5" Hows on to D.16.c.4.6. till

   Lift as follows

  (a) 2 4.5" Hows. on to D.23.d.0.8 till

  (b) 2. 4.5" Hows. on to D.23.a.5.9. till

  (c) 2 4.5" Hows. on to D.16.a.7.8. till

4. <u>D/242.</u>

  (a) 0.0 4 4.5" Hows. (SMOKE) D.27.d.1.9. –
       D.27.b.3.3.   till 0.

    This Screen is to smother the North
    end of LA PLAIGNE with smoke to confuse
    and harass the enemy holding it.

       <u>Estimated Expenditure.</u> 110 B.S.

  0. Lift as follows (H.E.)

  (i) 2 4.5" Hows. on to D.21.d.1.5. till

  (ii) 1 4.5" How. on to D.21.c.7.8. till

  (iii) 1 4.5" How. on to D.21.a.9.0. till

   Lift /

3.

Lift as follows

(i)   2   4.5" Hows. on to D.21.d.8.6.   till

(ii)   1   4.5" How.   on to D.22.a.0.0.   till

(iii) 1   4.5" How.   on to D.16.c.8.2.   till

Lift as follows

(i)   2   4.5" Hows. on to D.17.c.0.8   till

(ii)   1   4.5" How.   on to D.17.a.9.8.   till

(iii) 1   4.5" How.   on to D.16.b.9.1.   till

(b)   0.0   2   4.5" Hows. (SMOKE)   High ground round Chapel D.22.c.6.9.   till

Estimated Expenditure.   200 B.S.

Lift on to D.17.c.4.7. (H.E.)   till

The last co-ordinate given in every case will be the S.O.S. Lines for the Howitzers indicated.

5. Rates of Fire.

Rates of Fire throughout will be 2 rounds per How. per min.

APPENDIX "C".

1. 6" Newton Stokes Mortars will be put into action as follows:-

	No. of pieces.	Locality.	Objectives
(a)	2	J.10.central.	J.11.a.2.6.
(b)	2	J.9.d.6.6.	J.4.c.9.6.
(c)	1	J.9.d.6.6.	J.4.a.1.2.
(d)	2	D.25.b.6.4.	D.26.b.4.0.
(e)	1	D.25.b.6.4.	D.26.b.8.9.

2. Fire will be opened on "Z" Day at 0.0 and will lift off the objectives as follows :-

    (a)

    (b)

    (c)

    (d)

    (e)

Appendix D

Heavy Artillery Support required by
58th Division for proposed operation.

1. **5 8" Howitzers.**

   (a) O.O 2 8" Hows. on FORT de FLINES (101 fuze)
                                                     till 1.30

   (b) O.O 1 8" How. J.4.a.2.0. Two rounds in quick succession with 101 fuze; then lift to E.25.d.5.7. and search road down to bridge at E.25.d.8.6. with 106 fuze

   (c) O.O 1 8" How. J.3.b.9.2. Two rounds in quick succession with 101 fuze; then lift to D.30.b.0.7. and search the road and high ground up to entrance to wood E.19.c.0.2. with 106 fuze
                                                     till 1.30

   (d) O.O 1 8" How. D.21.a.7.0. with 106 fuze
                                                     till 0.4

         0.4 Lift on to D.22.a.6.0. and search high ground round Chapel with 106 fuze
                                                     till 1.20

         1.20 Lift on to D.17.d.1.9. with 106 fuze
                                                     till 1.45

   The Final Objectives for these Howitzers will be their S.O.S. Lines.

2. **11 6" Howitzers.**

   (a) O.O 2 6" Hows. open on J.5.c.2.9. - J.4.b.6.2. with 106 fuze   till

         Lift on to J.6.a.2.2. (1 How.) and J.6.c.5.7. (1 How.)   till

         Lift on to K.1.c.8.2. and E.25.d.0.0 till

   (b) O.O 4 6" Hows. Three rounds in succession on to J.3.b.9.0 - J.3.b.5.6. Then lift on to D.28.b.2.0., D.28.b.5.0., D.29.a.1.2. and D.29.d.0.3. (1 How. each)   till

         Lift on to E.19.a.3.5. (2 Hows.) D.24.a.6.2. (1 How.) and D.24.d.5.5. (1 How.)   till

   (c) O.O 1 6" How. on D.27.d.5.8.)
             2 6" Hows. on D.27.d.0.8) with 106 fuze.
                                                     till

         Lift on to D.28.a.5.6. (2 Hows.)
                      D.28.d.8.1 (1 How.)   till

         Lift on to D.22.a.2.3. (1 How)
                      D.18.c.0.5. (1 How)
                      D.17.c.8.2. (1 How.

   (d) /

2.

(d) O.O 1 6" How. on D.20.d.9.8.   till
           Lift on to D.21.a.6.1.   till
           Lift on to D.17.b.8.0.   till

(e) O.O 1 6" How. on to D.20.b.8.2.   till
           Lift on to D.21.a.7.4.   till
           Lift on to D.17.b.0.3.   till

The Final Objectives for these Howitzers will be their S.O.S. Lines.

3. (a) 1 60-pounder   Bridge E.15.d.2.8.
   (b) 1 60-pounder   Bridge E.22.a.1.9.

APPENDIX "E".

Ammunition to be dumped at positions.

1. Ammunition dumps will be begun on X/Y night and must be carefully camouflaged.

2. The amounts to be in all positions by 0.0 hours on Zero Day in excess of the echelons, which must all be full, will be as follows :-

18-pounder.   per gun.   225 Shrapnel.
                               75 H.E.
                               20 Smoke.

4.5" How.   per How.   200 H.E.

In addition to this amount, Smoke and Gas Shell will be distributed as follows :-

D/108   520 rounds B.S.
                              100   "   C.G.

D/242   310   "   B.S.

D/291   170   "   B.S.

Army Form C. 2118.

WAR DIARY
or
INTELLIGENCE SUMMARY.
(Erase heading not required.)

Instructions regarding War Diaries and Intelligence Summaries are contained in F. S. Regs. Part II. and the Staff Manual respectively. Title pages will be prepared in manuscript.

WO 24

Headquarters, 58th Divisional Artillery.

Place	Date	Hour	Summary of Events and Information	Remarks and references to Appendices
PERUWELZ. BELGIUM.			**December 1918.**	
	Dec. 2nd.		The 58th Division was inspected by General Sir H.S. HORNE, K.C.B., K.C.M.G., Commanding First Army, and the 58th Divisional Artillery were complimented for their smartness in drill and turnout.	
	-do-		Brigadier General J.Mc.C.MAXWELL, C.B., D.S.O., C.R.A., 58th Division, returned from 14 days special leave to the U.K.	
	Dec. 5th.		His Majesty King George V visited the Divisional Area.	
			Recreational and Educational Training was carried out during the month, and Demobilization commenced.	
			The dispositions of the Divisional Artillery are as under:-	
			H.Q.R.A. ... PERUWELZ.	
			290th Bde. RFA.	
			H.Q. & B & C Batteries. ... QUEVAUCAMPS.	
			"A" & "D" Batteries. BLATON.	
			291st Bde. RFA.	
			H.Q. & Batteries. ... BELOEIL.	
			58th Div.Ammn.Col. ... GRANDGLISE.	

Maxwell

Brigadier General,
C.R.A., 58th Division.

Index........................

SUBJECT.

8 KOYLI

No.	Contents.	Date.

www.ingramcontent.com/pod-product-compliance
Lightning Source LLC
Chambersburg PA
CBHW062359230426
43662CB00038B/2086